Advancing
for
Kingdom Sake!

SHELIA R. PEARSON

Advancing for Kingdom Sake!

Shelia R. Pearson

Copyright © 2020. Shelia Pearson. All rights reserved.

Advancing for Kingdom Sake!

DEDICATIONS

I would like to dedicate this book to my Heavenly Father, who has called and anointed me to inspire His people through skillful writings. This book would not have manifested without You empowering me to be all that You have anointed me to be. Thank You so much for allowing me to impart into the lives of your people.

To my spiritual parents, Apostle Jonathan and Prophetess Jessica Davis - thank you for being my kingdom examples. You all have imparted within me the spiritual drive that every apostolic leader needs. Thank you for encouraging me to maintain a steady momentum in the spirit.

Advancing for Kingdom Sake!

Acknowledgements

To my loving husband, Keith D. Pearson, Sr. and our three wonderful children; Kelvineisha, Kimberly and Keith, Jr.: *Thank you for believing in me and encouraging me throughout my journey as a writer.*

To my prayer partners all over the world: *Thank you all for standing in the gap with me over the years and for allowing me to share my passion for intercession with you.*

To my sister Kimberly Taylor: *Thank you for listening and encouraging me over the years. You have weathered many storms with me and I am grateful.*

To my sister Tiffany Blackmon: *Thank you for showing me so much love and commitment over the years and I am thankful to call you my prayer partner, my sister and friend.*

Advancing for Kingdom Sake!

FOREWORD

We live in a society that is starving and indeed suffering from the absence of knowledge in the areas of prayer and intercession, and it shows! *"Advancing for Kingdom Sake!"* presents immeasurable opportunities for rejection, repentance and reconciliation - all threaded together with grace in such a way that the reader is brought into a mature state of intercession with ease.

Upon reading, you will find yourself wanting to engage more into prayer and practice — with disciplines, habits, and patterns for an effectual and fervent prayer life. Beginning with the title all the way through to the final word you will be pricked, purged, provoked, and pushed into deep realms of intercession. It will stir up a strong passion for unity, love, and obedience for the glory of God.

Rarely have I been engaged by a piece of work as I am by Author Shelia Pearson's wisdom and revelation of intercession. Each time I opened it to read a few pages, I found that I could not stop. I told myself, *"Just one more page,"* but inevitably I kept on reading. Part of the exquisite beauty of this book is that you will want to read it again and again because it is filled with so much apostolic prophetic information, impartation, and inspiration for intercessors globally.

I love this book because the writer, Shelia Pearson, allows people to open themselves to the silent power of grace and forgiveness resulting in profound physical, emotional and spiritual healing through her testimony.

- This book matures the spirit.
- This book feeds the soul that is seeking healing.
- This book is a tried-and-true prayer guide through the dark paths of life. Each chapter is an enlightened piece of work that is an essential read for all people who are truly devoted to the care and refinement of their souls and call to intercession.

Finally, it is a great book on prayer that is filled with personal, biblical, and practical truth to help generate a culture of prayer - both in you and those around you. It encourages you to have faith like Abraham, wisdom like Solomon, and tenacity like Daniel. Shelia shows us that to pray is to see Jesus more clearly and meet Him more regularly in every single aspect and moment of our lives. I feel privileged to write the foreword for Author Shelia Pearson not just because I believe so strongly in intercessory prayer, but ultimately because I've witnessed the power of intercession work in her life continually. Her life shows true commitment to the kingdom of God as an apostolic prophetic intercessor and I am honored to know her.

Thanks, daughter, for calling us back to what really matters!

- Jessica Selvy-Davis

Shelia R. Pearson

Advancing for Kingdom Sake!

Shelia R. Pearson

CONTENTS

Foreword

Introduction — *A God Given Quest*

Chapter 1 — *Demonstrating the God Kind of Love*

Chapter 2 — *The Power of Intercession*

Chapter 3 — *Facing the Real Enemy*

Chapter 4 — *Faith and Fear*

Chapter 5 — *Whispers of Lies*

Chapter 6 — *The Power of Love*

Chapter 7 — *The Fear of Rejection*

Chapter 8 — *Dethroning Satan*

Chapter 9 — *Enough is Enough!*

Chapter 10 — *Taking Your Exalted Seat*

Chapter 11 — *Blazing a Trial of Righteousness*

Chapter 12 — *The Ongoing Battle*

Chapter 13 — *The Power to Start and Finish*

Conclusion — *A Kingdom Display*

Advancing for Kingdom Sake!

Shelia R. Pearson

Introduction

A God Given Quest

I chose my second book to get into more details of the things I've suffered while on this quest for unity. All of the things that I've been through have strengthened me enough to accept my role as Apostolic Intercessor. It is an amazing assignment to be called to intercede and reestablish the gifts that God has ordained to edify and build up His Church. Over the years, I have embraced many different denominations, only that I may see and deal with the tactics of the enemy. I must say that I have encountered more division and competition in the body than I can ever write or preach about. However, I am wise enough to know that every encounter was sent to help me fully understand who I am in the realm of the spirit.

Now that I have been given this enlightened truth about myself, I can better appreciate my unique and unfailing compassion to cover God's chosen vessels. Once you begin to understand your role for the body of Christ, the peace of God becomes your abiding place. Peace is found in the place of your God given identity. Regardless of the many titles I am called to cover in prayer; Apostle, Prophet, Evangelist, Pastor, Teacher, Bishop, Overseer, Elder, Missionary etc., none of these anointed titles identify me like the gift of intercession. It is a gift that is often overlooked and rejected, but it is ordained by God to cover all. I thank God for bringing simplicity to my calling and assignment.

It is a delight to be recognized as an intercessor—someone who stands in the gap on the behalf of others. Someone who is empowered to love and show compassion for God's creation. Someone who has been given the ability to bring forth the perfect will of God in the earth. It is my desire that my assignment will help others walk in the fullness of who they are. A walk that will free them from the limitations that were meant to hinder them. A walk that will also deliver them from questioning their own unique abilities.

This is an awakening moment in time for me. I am aware that a mandate has been placed on my life to draw the body of Christ into a life of intercession. I know that obedience is a requirement to receive all that God has for me and writing this book is one of my acts of obedience. It is my prayer that after you read this book, you will see your level of understanding and then work on all the necessary changes to become fully developed in the things of God. As I write this to intercessors, know that I am reaching out to believers. The Bible didn't address intercession as a call for some but we are all called to pray without ceasing. We will truly miss out on the power that God has made available to His body if we continue thinking that intercessors are a few wailing women picked out to pray until something happens.

There is no way of preparing for a life of intercession without understanding that the Holy Spirit partners with the Saints during this process of prayer. This fact is proven in Romans 8:27-28 (AMP.) It states, *"And He Who searches the hearts of men knows what is in the mind of the [Holy] Spirit [what His intent is], because the Spirit intercedes and pleads [before God] in behalf of the **Saints** according to and in harmony with God's will. We are assured and know that **[God being a partner in their labor]** all things work together and are [fitting into a plan] for good **to and for those who love God and are called according to [His] design and purpose.**"

The key thing to understand is that you are a **Saint, you are filled with His Spirit** and you are partnering with the All-Knowing God. It is always His desire to work through His people to get the needed results. We must enter into intercession knowing that because we are in Him, all things are working together according to His plan.

Reader, it is my desire that this written material would equip you to stand firm in the things of God. I pray that standing firm would become your posture in the spirit and wavering would become a thing of the past. I pray that every man, woman, boy and girl will grow in the capacity needed in every season of their lives. I come against premature growth and immature pauses in the spirit. I pray that God would increase you in ways a natural mind will never understand. It is my prayer that you would read this book with great passion and put God's holy angels to work in your life. God is ready to use you as an instrument of His glory and I pray that you would become sensitive enough to receive all that He has for you.

Shelia R. Pearson

From My Heart to Yours

It is important that you hear God especially when it comes to your kingdom assignment. There are many gifts and administrations but God has anointed you to do a specific work for His kingdom. It is easy to be tossed about by many winds of doctrines, but when you have an ear to hear what the spirit of God is saying to the church, you will never be sidetracked. Your hearing abilities will always posture you in a place to be governed by God and Him alone. Opening your ears to Him will keep you on the path to get the results you were born to receive. You will also have proper discernment as you walk in the power of prayer. So, it is my prayer that you stay on your quest designed for you and that God will give you a steady momentum to do your kingdom assignment according to His plan in Jesus name.

Advancing for Kingdom Sake!

CHAPTER 1

Demonstrating the God Kind of Love

"EAGERLY PURSUE and seek to acquire[this] love [make it your aim, your great quest]; and earnestly desire and cultivate the spiritual endowments (gifts), especially that you may prophesy (interpret the divine will and purpose in inspired preaching and teaching." (1Corinthians 1:14 AMP). As intercessors, we must keep our priorities straight. This word encourages us to eagerly pursue the main thing, which is love. There is no way we will function as Christ partners in prayer if we fail to demonstrate His love. The next instructions given tells us to cultivate the gifts that are given, especially that you may prophesy. The prophetic is what identifies us as intercessors. We are given the ability to interpret the divine will and purpose of God. Yes, this is just as powerful as it sounds, but we must keep our love walk right. Intercession is a work of the Spirit of God and He will never dwell in a temple that is not releasing His love and integrity.

It is vital that we truly see how the enemy continues to gain control in our lives. We walk into this life of salvation full of zeal, power and love. But once the test and trials hit our lives, we begin serving God on the surface. Our mouths are professing love but our hearts are far from demonstrating it. We find ourselves caught up in doing church work but we fail horribly at demonstrating the God of the church. We serve a God of love and love has become a diminishing gift. This is not the plan of God and it most definitely doesn't demonstrate the heart of God. How can we do the work of Christ if we fail to display His character? Once we begin going after titles and denominations, the love walk turns into a walk of competition.

"Advancing for Kingdom Sake!" wasn't birthed out until I started evangelizing and seeing the heart condition of men and women claiming to be called, anointed and appointed for kingdom works. Now there is no way of representing anything if you fail to imitate it in Word and in deed. We as believers are called to release the "even greater works" that Jesus mentions in the Scriptures. But this will not manifest if we never learn to become imitators of Christ. We should be loving like Him, talking like Him and daily walking like Him. There is no way of pretending to be anointed by God. The real anointing will always release and demonstrate God's unadulterated truth.

The message that God has anointed me to deliver is not a popular one. It has a way of placing me on a field of war. I am called to deal with the false representation of the kingdom of God. Well of course this means I don't have many friends and the ones I once viewed as friends have walked away due to my delivery of the truth. All I can say is that I would rather lose friends than my direct contact with the heart of God. I know that I didn't lose friends because I failed to demonstrate the love of God. I lost them because I refused to compromise. We must pursue the things of God with everything within us and we must also be consumed with the love of God to truly demonstrate His character.

We have been filled with God so that we can work great exploits for His kingdom. To do great works for the kingdom of God, we must speak truth regardless of the enemies that might manifest during the process. Jesus declared, *"But when He, the Spirit of Truth (the Truth-giving Spirit) comes, he will guide you into all the Truth (the whole, full Truth). For He will not speak His own message [on His own authority];*

but He will tell whatever He hears [from the Father]; He will give the message that has been given to Him], and He will announce and declare to you the things that are to come [that will happen in the future." (St. John 16:13 AMP). Our assignments must become unapologetic. We have enough gossip in the world, it is time we allow the oil of God to flow from the pulpit! How can we expect to go into all the world making a difference, if we fail to preach the Gospel? We must take on the same mind of Christ, telling the people whatever we hear from the Father. This must become the attitude of every believer striving to be kingdom minded. We cannot allow the cares of the world to hinder our progress in the kingdom. We must stay focused and press forward, demonstrating nothing but the God kind of love.

In St John 15:1-5 AMP Jesus proclaims, *"I am the True Vine, and My Father is the Vinedresser. Any branch in me that does not bear fruit [that stops bearing] he cuts away (trims off, take away); and He cleanses and repeatedly prunes every branch that continues to bear fruit."* In verse five he goes on expressing who we are in Him and what He expects of us. *"I am the Vine; you are the branches. Whoever lives in Me and I in him bears much (abundant) fruit."* I shared these verses to highlight the importance of truly releasing the kingdom way. God expects us to reproduce His kind. As intercessors, it is our job to bring forth for God. We must learn to draw from the True Vine to the point that all man can see is the truth of God coming forth. Our words must become the Words that God speaks. If we are declaring that we are children of God, we must always represent Him in all that we do and in all that we say.

I was once privileged to hear my spiritual mother speak a powerful message. She taught on the importance of becoming a powerful church again. The Word was so profound because she answered a very important question, *"Why has the church become a powerless one?"* This is one question that every leader should be asking themselves. There is no way of advancing God's kingdom without having His power. The house of God has shifted into an 'I can do it my way' kind of house. God has not made His Holy Spirit available to us to ignore His way of doing things. We can't live unproductive lives and still enjoy the benefits of eating the good of the land. The benefits of heaven are granted only when we learn to demonstrate the lives that heaven demands. This starts with the teachings that Jesus taught, *"Love your neighbor as yourself."* This is one of the greatest commandments and we are failing at the neighborly love on extreme levels. But I must admit that the "loving yourself" part of this command is demonstrated quite well. To receive the power to continue the work that Jesus demonstrated, we must get our love walk right. The key things to know about God's love is that it has nothing to do with you, but everything to do with the fellowmen.

The word charity means love, benevolence, and goodwill; the disposition of heart which inclines men to think favorably of their fellowmen (KJV Dictionary). Love is free from any form of prejudice; it radiates out as a universal release. This word universal means no one is excluded regardless of gender, race, culture, denomination gift or talent. To advance a kingdom that belongs to God we must learn to imitate His standards and His standards can only be demonstrated through His love.

Once we have mastered this love walk, His Spirit will lead us into all truth.

The Word teaches us that if, *"We can speak in the tongues of men and [even] of angels, but have not love (the reasoning, intentional, spiritual devotion such as inspired by God's love for and in us), we are only noisy gongs and clanging symbols. And if we have prophetic powers (and understand all the secrets, truths and mysteries and possess all knowledge, and if we have (sufficient) faith so that we can remove mountains but have not love (God's love in us) we are nothing (useless no bodies)."* Our gifts alone are not powerful enough to work great exploits for God's kingdom, but love is the one gift that describes the fullness of God. It is the only gift that can identify you with God. The Word teaches us that *"The one who does not love has not become acquainted with God [does not and never did know Him], for God is Love."* (1 John 4:8 AMP). We as intercessors are called and appointed to represent God in the fullness of His power and the only way to accomplish this is demonstrating His love.

Shelia R. Pearson
Maintaining A Servant's Heart

It has always been my desire to serve and the enemy has fought against me serving for so many years. Even the enemy knows that serving empowers you to do ministry God's way. It gives you the integrity and humility that elevates you into new realms of authority. I have had the opportunity to sit under many leaders and to my surprise, I was rejected and even instructed to start my own church. My level of warfare has been serious only because I was an anointed vessel that wanted to serve. I always joined ministries in a spirit of humility but as intercessor, I've always had an eye to see every exalted seat of the enemy. A true servant is given the eye to see the enemy in all his forms and manifestations. They are also given the boldness to put their finger on him regardless of who he chooses to manifest himself through.

I can remember serving as an intercessory prayer leader in one ministry. I was instructed to pray for an upcoming revival and God began uncovering the enemy through one of the guest speakers. I prayed for all the leaders on the program but one of the speakers had a strong level of negative intent. God began revealing to me that his heart was totally against my pastor and it was best I warn him. I took this revelation to my pastor and I was surprised about the response that I received. He really didn't allow me to get into details before completely shutting me down. I was really messed up in my spirit about how he handled that valuable information. Even though he failed to respond properly, I didn't allow it to shift me off my prayer assignment. I continued to pray against the tactics of the enemy and I shared all the detail information with another intercessor in the church. I shared with her the heart condition of the guest speaker and I also shared with her that he would back out at the last minute. I couldn't share this information with the person that really needed to know this because he was too prideful to listen. I must say that I maintained my servant's attitude and God exalted me. The leader backed out at the last minute just as the Lord had revealed to me. I didn't have to say anything because my prayer partner shared all the detail information about this prayer assignment with my pastor. She told him that I had forewarned her that the speaker would back out because he had a negative intent from the beginning. I am sure that my pastor felt bad and a little embarrassed about how he handled me but to God be the glory!

I eventually left this church and joined another ministry in the city. After serving a few months at my new church, I was led to share my vision with the pastor. I typed up a long letter explaining my assignment for the city at that time. After my pastor read the letter, I was asked to leave his church and obey God. He explained to me that anything with two heads is a devil and it was best that I leave. I felt as if my heart had literally dropped out of my chest. I know that my vision is great but it does not exalt me into a seat so high that I can't be covered by leadership. I know that my vision is a very powerful mandate that needs to remain under the covering of true spiritual leaders. These are some of the things I've experienced as an apostolic intercessor for God's kingdom. I am proud to say that I didn't allow the rejection to stagnate me when it came to my love walk. It is my prayer that leaders will learn how to love God's people regardless of the diversity of their gifts. Believers and unbelievers alike need to experience the God kind of love and it most definitely should be demonstrated in the church.

Shelia R. Pearson

From My Heart to Yours

God has filled you with His love to make an impact in this world. The love of God is overflowing through you to flow on others. God has anointed you to see things before they happen. You are also empowered to shift things in the spirit. This sensitivity of the move of God is not always understood and this is why books like this need to manifest. You are different because you are anointed to birth out the will of God in the earth realm. You are overflowing with the love that every believer should have and it is my prayer that you never shift off your love walk. God has anointed me as Apostolic Intercessor to help you see yourself through His eyes. He has anointed you and you are different to make a supernatural difference in this natural realm.

Chapter 2

The Power of Intercession

There are certain requirements that we must meet to experience the true power of intercession. The main thing we must know is that intercession is a holy calling. To function in this level of power, we must house the Spirit of God. This anointed release gives us a *God conscious*. It reaches down into the core of our beings, bringing out hearts of repentance. It shifts us into a transparent state, releasing nothing but wonder working power. The power that heals sick bodies and saves the souls of men. The Bible explains it this way, "……*the heartfelt and persistent prayer of a righteous man (believer) can accomplish much [when put into action and made effective by God it is dynamic and can have tremendous power]."* (James 5:16 AMP).

The Holy Spirit meets us in our times of prayer and begins to take us up in the spirit. He releases through us the needed prayer which delivers the results that makes a tremendous difference. **Once the manifested glory of God enters our time of prayer, it shifts it from a simple prayer to a time of intercession. This is the power that the church is missing in this day and time and it will quickly return once we learn to allow the love of God to usher us into true intercession.**

We have learned the importance of being filled with the Holy Spirit. The Bible teaches us that during intercession, *"the Spirit Himself goes to meet our supplication and pleads in our behalf with unspeakable yearnings and groanings too deep for utterance"* (Romans 8:26 AMP). This is the one manifestation of intercession that brings confusion. The sound of intercession is powerful only when brought on by the Spirit of God Himself. We can't start and stop a travail in the natural and we most definitely can't start or stop one in the spirit! It is so important that we understand this scripture. I say this because I have witnessed leaders attempting to lead their congregation into intercession and the people of God are asked to wail out of their spirits. During this time, the sound of intercession fills the building but not the power of intercession. This is truth because intercession is 100% a work of the Spirit and it will never manifest through the flesh. It cannot be brought on by human emotions. God allows us to partner with Him in intercession, and during this process we encounter how He feels about any given situation; it may be the heart felt tears that brings life into a dead situation or the wrath of God that pushes back the forces of evil.

Once you are filled with the Spirit of God, He begins to use you to birth out His will. You may see this taking place in the midst of a prophetic release. There are times when God places an urgency on His Word - meaning the minute that it is released, an intercessor catches that prophetic release and begins giving birth immediately; this too can only manifest as the Spirit moves upon the intercessor. These different manifestations of intercession are often viewed as weird and misunderstood and this is why it must become written material. God desires to work miracles in the mist of us but we must take the limits off. God's way of doing things are way beyond our limited thinking and it is time that we let Him have free course. The people of God need to become more aware of the different ways that God moves prophetically through His people.

Becoming Spiritually Drawn!

Intercession has a way of leading the believer into a life lived in the Spirit. We are drawn into true intimacy with the Father. Intercessors are vessels who have put their minds, will, and emotions under the subjection of the Holy Spirit. The spiritual side becomes the governing factor, demolishing completely the deeds of the flesh. They understand that they are called to a life of being inwardly drawn into a deeper revelation of who they are through the shed blood of Christ. They are trained to put away the former desires; the cravings that manifest a carnal nature.

Embracing this spiritually drawn lifestyle requires a made-up mind - a mind that declares victory regardless of the wrestle. This is the life that commands the believer to move forward towards becoming fully developed in the things of God. It is a process of growth that walks the believer out of the outer court and into the holy place. It is important that we strive for advancement in the Kingdom of God. The Bible encourages us to *"Get past the elementary stage in the teaching and doctrine of Christ (the Messiah), advancing steadily toward the completeness and perfection that belongs to spiritual maturity."* (Hebrews 6:1 AMP). God is in the business of elevating His people. He expects us to get past the repentant stage. He wants us to purify our hearts with desires to experience the holy of holies. This is the level of power that every believer should want to experience. We should desire to house the Holy One with true demonstrations of His power working through us.

Shelia R. Pearson

Why do we ask the Spirit to live in our hearts, if we have no desire to become true temples of God? Accepting Jesus places a command on us to get rid of the formal lifestyle. We must change our way of thinking by hearing and applying the Word of God to our daily lives. We are encouraged to, *"Get rid of all uncleanness and the rampant outgrowth of wickedness; and in a humble (gentle, modest) spirit, receive and welcome the Word - which implanted and rooted [in our hearts] contains the power to save our souls."* (James 1:21 AMP). Advancement requires us becoming rooted and grounded in the Word of God. The Word goes on to tell us that the Word must be heard and applied; it states, *"But be doers of the Word [obey the message], and not merely listeners to it, betraying yourselves [into deception by reasoning contrary to the Truth]."* (James 1:22 AMP).

We are only deceiving ourselves when we sit under the power of the Word and continue living contrary lives. We should desire the manifested glory of God to be evident in our lives. Once we learn to live this life of righteousness, we will reap the fruit of our doings. The Bible explains it this way, *"For he who looks carefully into the faultless law, the [law] of liberty, and is faithful to it and perseveres in looking into it, being not a heedless listener who forgets but an active doer [who obeys], he shall be blessed in his doings (his life of obedience)."* (James 1:25 AMP). I have enough faith to believe that everything written in the Bible is true. If we live the life that God commands, the benefits of righteousness will overtake us! I cannot end this chapter without sharing these final instructions from James 4:7-10 AMP. It encourages us to be subject to God. *"Resist the devil [Stand firm against him], and he will flee from you.*

Come close to God and He will come close to you. [Recognize that you are] sinners, get your soiled hands clean; [realize that you have been disloyal] wavering individuals with divided interest and purify your heart [of your spiritual adultery]. [As you draw near to God] be deeply penitent and grieve, even weep [over your disloyalty]. Let your laughter be turned to grief and your mirth to dejection and heart felt shame [for your sins]. Humble yourselves [feel very insignificant] in the presence of the Lord and he will exalt you [He will lift you up and make your lives significant]."

Shelia R. Pearson

From My Heart to Yours

The life we live in this flesh is choice driven. We can choose to reject the flesh and walk daily in the spirit. We can also choose to live daily in our flesh and miss out on all of the many blessings that God has predestined for us. It is my prayer that you choose wisely. I pray that you embrace the truth of this Word and live victoriously in Christ. Keep in mind that you must become inwardly drawn by the Spirit of God to function as a believer. You must also present yourself to God holy to be used as an intercessor in this hour. And know that it is a powerful gift to become a vessel used to manifest God's will in the earth.

Advancing for Kingdom Sake!

CHAPTER 3

Facing the Real Enemy!

Upon writing this book the world is facing the greatest pandemic known to man. Fear has become the dominating factor and all I can hear the Lord saying to me is, *"Write about this monster of a spirit."* It is not hard to obey God in this command. It is actually my pleasure to point the enemy out. He has made the decision to boldly enter into my personal space. It is strange that he would try me on this level due to my history with him, I am a woman of intense warfare. He has always been on his job and after so many years of battling with him, I have learned to deal with him on the level expected of me. I know not to waver when it comes to my bold standing posture. As I stand therefore in the Spirit, God continues to allow me to see my enemy. The more I teach about his tactics, the more he makes himself visible. I will never forget the night I came face to face with him. As I closed my eyes to sleep, I saw him lurking in the darkness. The more I pointed him out, the more bold he became. During these grand appearances, it seemed as if my invisible foe was gradually gaining a foothold in my life. The reality of this made me question God. It was hard to understand why fear had entered my life on such a great level. The Lord explained that He had to allow me to undergo the same level of fear that a lot of His people were experiencing. Fear had to become a visible enemy so that I could really shine light on the truth.

    I can hear the Lord commanding me to explain to His people the danger of allowing fear to get a grip on their lives. He's saying, *"Bring to light the different ways he enters their lives; show them how he captivates their dreams. Tell them the power he gains over their lives simply because they fail to know how real he is."* God wanted me to understand that I wasn't shining a light on fear so that the devil might win some brownie points. But He stated, *"You are writing this book to do what you are called to do—snatch souls out of the clutches of the enemy's demonic grip."* I am aware that many are afraid of their own thoughts, some are afraid to sleep due to this dreadful monster making himself visible. There are people resting only to enter dreams where the enemy is stalking them. God is commanding me to write about an invisible foe that has been given access to destroy so many lives.

The spirit of fear is more than what most people view him as. He is viewed as an entity because this is how real he is. He has a distinct personality and he finds his existence in the heart of man. People everywhere must understand that there is a force behind this spirit working to destroy all that God has created man to be. How can we demonstrate dominion if we fear the very things that God has given us power over? The first commandments given from the Creator has found a resting place in the aisle of fear, every turn is blocked back darkness. As I obey God in writing this truth, light is being surrounded by this enemy that continues to go unnoticed.

It is my prayer that my obedience in writing this book will open eyes that have been blind folded by the enemy. I declare that as this material is being read, demonic scales are falling off the eyes of believers everywhere. Fear will no longer gain the power and authority that has been given to man. No longer will the enemy be given access to rule areas that God has given man to have dominion over. I speak life to every lifeless soul and I declare that the resurrected power of the Word is commanding you to rise again. Rise from the pain of your past hurts. Rise from the fear of the unknown. Rise from the fear of doing you just the way

God anointed you to do you. A resurrected dream is coming back within view. A resurrected marriage is filled with the love and passion that it was meant to have. A resurrected singer is singing melodies that will save souls. A resurrected writer is becoming the author they were born to be. All of this is taking place because a real enemy called "Fear" is being exposed on the greatest level of exposure.

A Spiritual Disturbance

The morning I started writing this chapter, I was awakened from a dream. In the dream, my husband and I were really enjoying each other. The room was filled with so much joy and laughter. During this exciting moment, I looked up and saw a demonic spirit walking towards us. A strong spirit of fear gripped my heart and when I opened my eyes, I heard the Lord commanding me to bring exposure. God was giving me a peaceful moment in my dream due to the fact that my husband was out of town. He had been away on a business trip for weeks and God was allowing me to enjoy him through a dream.

The enemy sends disturbance to counteract the plans of God. He sends chaos in the midst of peaceful situations. He works with a persistent effort to divide what God has unified; notice how he manifested himself in the garden of Eden. Adam and Eve lived a perfect life but yet the enemy found a way to disturb the tranquility of man. He showed up in the very first marriage and he is still showing up today. As couples grow in their love walk, they will learn more and more about one another. There will be good days and bad days. It is the enemy's desire that we remain in the bad. He reminds us of past hurts to the point of blinding us to our future. Fear takes giant steps into our lives by leading us into building walls. These defense mechanisms are used to stop us from progressing. The walls of defense keep us from seeing past the damage and we find ourselves stagnated in life. There is no vision for the future because all we can see is the pain of our past. During this time we find ourselves living in the "what if" of life. *"What if I forgive my husband and he end up hurting me again?*

What if I make plans with him and he leaves me for someone else? What if I love him anyway and he finds ways to show me that I was a foolish wife?

The only way to defeat this invisible enemy is learning to operate in the Spirit. The Word of God reassures us that, *"God has not given us a spirit of timidity or cowardice or fear, but [He has given us a spirit] of power and of love and a sound judgement and personal discipline [abilities that result in a calm, well-balanced mind and self-control."* (1 Timothy 1:7 AMP). We entered into union with our spouses because we loved them. It is important that we know that love and fear can't operate together. Love will cast out fear or fear will cast out love. The Bible states that, *"There is no fear in love [dread does not exist]. But perfect (complete, full grown) love drives out fear, because fear involves [the expectation of divine] punishment, so the one who is afraid [of God's judgment] is not perfected in love [has not grown into a sufficient understanding of God's love]."* (1 John 4:18 AMP). The enemy understands that mastering love places our feet in a place that he will never experience. He also understands that fear keeps us from truly representing the God of love. I will highlight more about why the enemy targets our love walk in Chapter 6.

Shelia R. Pearson

From My Heart to Yours

The enemy is truly a master deceiver and it is my prayer that you know him. Once you are able to recognize his tactics, he will lose battles. He can only dominate in your life if you give him that power. God has empowered you as intercessor to keep the devil in his place of defeat. This is truth because God has filled you with Himself and He is also partnering with you in the spirit. Know that you are overflowing with the love of God and with the power of God. It is my prayer that you access your power of love and continue to demolish all the works of the devil.

CHAPTER 4

Faith and Fear

As I continue to bring the spirit of fear within view, the only image you will see is Satan. He is the ruler of this dark entity. Satan does his best work by captivating minds with fear. Once he is given access, he works in a persistent effort to keep God's people from functioning in faith. Just as love and fear can't function together neither can faith and fear. It is a tug of war situation and only one can win the battle. There is no in between — it is either faith or fear.

The Word tells us to cast down vain imaginations because the enemy does his best work in our minds (2 Corinthians 10:5 KJV). If our minds are given over to this deceiving spirit, he will paint images of falsity. The lies will feel so real and you will start responding to these false images of deception. This is how the spirit of fear destroy lives. If words of faith aren't released during these times, your mind becomes captivated. Satan will convince you to believe his lies and his way begins governing your way. This is another way he keeps us living in the pain of our past. There will always be something trivial that snatches your mind back into a matter that has been given over to God. You will have to be vigilant and cautious at all times because the enemy roams around seeking ways to keep you bound (1 Peter 5:8 KJV). He is totally aware of the fact that hell is his final and complete destination. He will never be given an opportunity to live the good life and he secretly uses his tactics to destroy the life that is predestined for you to live.

When God created man, he made our purpose for living very clear. We were to have dominion! This is the level of authority that God has given us and even though the enemy is real, we have to give him access to our domain. The promises of God must become the fuel that drives us. As we embrace the things of God, we are expected to become developed in our thinking. This can only manifest through giving ourselves substance to live by. The enemy gains ground in the lives of so many believers due to them seeking and searching for wisdom in all the wrong places. Wisdom can only be found in God. As we build our relationship with our Heavenly Father, it is His desire that we continue growing steadily in the things of the Spirit. During this process of growth, we are forced to leave some things behind. Lingering in the things of the past only gives the enemy access to gain more ground in our lives.

The Word and Fear

The Word of God has been given to keep you on your roads to success. As you continue to travel the ordained path of life, know that your adversary will always send his penetrating darts. This must be expected and making preparation for your enemy is paramount. As you continue growing, the enemy will fight against your standing power. During these times you are expected to keep in mind where your strength comes from. The Word of God encourages us to, *"Be strong in the Lord [to draw our strength from God and be empowered through our union with Him] and in the power of His [boundless] might."* (Ephesians 6:10 AMP). Our strength comes from a God that cannot be defeated.

One of the greatest weapons given to combat our enemy is the Word of God. It must be viewed as the only substance for survival. It is an absolute power, meaning there is no need to add or take away from it. Once we make the decision to give ourselves wholly to the Word, the necessary changes will manifest. A reconstruction takes place from within, birthing out the new creatures we were born to be. We are *"Born again [that is, reborn from above—spiritually transformed, renewed, and set apart for God's purpose] not of seed which is perishable but [from that which is] imperishable and immortal, that is, through the living and everlasting Word of God."* (1Peter 1:23 AMP).

There is a security in God that we can stand on. He is faithful and He will never forsake us. It is not always easy to see how present our God is but our faith puts this truth within view. It does not matter about the attacks we encounter in this world; we are secured in the fact that we are in this world but we are not of this world. Speaking the Word regardless of the test gives us that reassurance that no weapon formed against us will be able to prosper (Isaiah 54:17 KJV). Faith gives us that confidence that fear or no other manifested spirit can overtake us. As we stand on faith and release the all-powerful Word of God, we will keep our enemy in his place of defeat. He is a persistent enemy and he will continue with the hope to find us slipping, but as long as we stand with a therefore stand, he will remain in his place of defeat—under our feet!

From My Heart to Yours

As Intercessor, you are expected to make your request known to God in faith, one hundred percent free of doubt. Know that once your mind is unstable concerning the promises of God, He places you in a category with doubters. You can only be classified as a person who cannot please God because of the uncertainty of the instructions given. It is impossible to move forward if you are indecisive about the direction you should be taking. God's instructions are always clear and He will not change His mind because you have allowed fear to overshadow your mind. It is time to shake off everything that is hindering you and put God's instruction right before you. His instructions will always point you to your purpose and you can only demonstrate a blessed life in Christ when you make intelligent decisions to press into your purpose for life.

Shelia R. Pearson

CHAPTER 5
Whispers of Lies

The enemy is known as the father of lies. The Word teaches us that when he speaks a lie, he speaks of his own nature: for he is a liar, and the father thereof (John 8:44). He is also a very cunning and crafty enemy. He finds ways to get access into the minds of believers. It is his job to keep you in a mindset of defeat. His main focus is to lure you off of the path of freedom. His snares of deceit start with his whispers of lies. He understands that the human mind feeds and grows on information, rather negative or positive. If you are given over to the painted images he puts before you, he wins. This is why it is a must that you cast down vain imaginations and every high thing that exalts itself against the knowledge of God (2 Corinthians 10:5). The enemy will continue presenting useless and unproductive things to entice us. It is always his desire to keep us from embracing the new and improved way. He understands that our new life in Christ is just that—new.

He uses his best weapons of deceit during the immature stage. He starts by telling us that God knows our hearts. He does this with an attempt to convince us that God will excuse our sins because He understands our weaknesses. Yes, God understands everything about us, but the enemy never paints the full picture. He shows us just enough to capture our attention with a hope that we would remain in bondage. I reiterate, God is aware of our weaknesses and He is even more aware of the power of His Word. The Bible tells us that, *"This then is the message which we have heard of Him, and declare unto you, that God is light, and in Him is no darkness at all."* (1John 1:5). We are encouraged to, *"Love not the world, neither the things that are in the world."* It goes on to teach us that, *"If any man loves the world, the love of the Father is not in him.*

For all that is in the world, the lust of the flesh, and the lust of the eyes, and the pride of life, is not of the Father, but is of the world." (1 John 2:15). It does not matter how long we've indulged ourselves in the things of the world, the light of God's precepts will completely change us. The more we give ourselves to the things of the spirit the more we become like God.

There is so much power in knowing who you are through God and how He expects you to view yourselves. It is equally important to believe the truth that you know. This is why a wavering mind is a dangerous mind. The enemy is a prowling enemy, looking for ways to enter into your domain. He needs a dark entrance way but your faith will only radiate the light of God. There are no penetrations from the darts of the enemy when faith has become your shield of protection. The enemy is aware of his final destination and he searches out ways to divert yours. This is why we must know the truth, stand on the truth, and release the truth each time we see our enemy.

Shelia R. Pearson

Targeting a Christ Aligned Mind

Life situations can come with great force and sometimes the impact leads us to detours instead of the path that is ordained for our lives. The pain of life experiences can put us in a mindset of guarding our hearts, and guarding our hearts is not a bad thing. It only becomes damaging when we refuse to open up to the things that are meant to get us to our appointed destinations. We find ourselves getting away from the true script. We start writing our own stories, leaving no room for God. This is dangerous because He is the only One Who can lead and guide us into all truth.

A damaged heart is in need of God's healing power and to receive from God, we must remain in His perfect will. He is a God of order and He will never force His righteous path upon us. It is a choice that we must make and God is always waiting on us to make the right decisions. Sometimes it is very difficult to make quality decisions due to the damage that has been done. The thing about a damaged heart is that it works with a persistent effort to stay out of harm's way. By all means necessary the individual will stay away from the places viewed as danger zones. But sometimes the things we view as danger zones are the things that God is trying to use to make us stronger.

Once God begins revealing His script for your life, there is nothing powerful enough to abort the process. He starts by making His instructions clear and all you can see are the detours and dead-end roads you chose to travel. You will see the many times you allowed your emotions to be the governing factor in your life. There is a difference between the path you chose and the chosen path given by God. Your path is dictated by the flesh and God's path has no room for the flesh. It is predetermined and there is no other route to take. Regardless of the turbulence along the way, you are reminded that you were built to last. God has a way of letting you know that His way is the only way.

The end result of traveling in the wrong direction is experiencing a devastating end. As Christians, we should be on a journey that leads to victory and the enemy shouldn't ever be given access to take our eyes off our God given instructions. Truth must be magnified greater than the pain of past hurts. Once we put truth in its rightful place, we are placed in a position to be governed by God's power. I can personally say that learning and operating in this truth has opened doors that no man can close in my life. At one time a disconnection had taken place in my life that had enough power to abort my process of growth. Even though it was clear that I was called to the church, I had no desire to be a part of it. I convinced myself that I could pray for the church from a distance. This is an example of staying away from the danger zones.

I must admit that this experience taught me that any slight shift from God's instructions will cause chaos and confusion. When God has given clear instructions, editing is not necessary. We have the tendency to try to avoid the potholes on our roads to success. We want the path to be free of discomfort but sometimes discomfort is necessary to bring out the best from within. It was the pain of my past that caused me to guard my heart with all diligence. It was hard to connect with anyone because the trust I had for leadership had disappeared. The old had wrapped itself around me like a garment. Receiving and releasing love was impossible because I had my guards up. This level of thinking went on for years. Even though wisdom was screaming, *"Plant yourself,"* it felt safer to run away from the pain of my past. God's voice was loud and clear but my damaged heart made it very difficult to stay rooted and grounded in truth.

The enemy tries your faith on a daily basis and through his craftiness, he persuades you to agree with him. Once your actions shift off true alignment, he gains a foothold in your lives. Keep in mind that he is after your domain because he understands the dominion that has been given to you. The enemy does not want temporary control, he wants total and complete control. He does not waste his time with small matters, he targets the pure in heart. Filtration is the dark power he functions in. He knows that a removal of truth must take place in order for him to have victory in any given situation. This is why the mind can never be given over to his lies of deceit.

The whole of man must be given over to the ways and purposes of God - this includes the soul, body and spirit of man. Once you come into the knowledge of the truth, it must be a truth that remains. *"You must present your bodies [dedicating all of yourselves, set apart] as a living sacrifice, holy and well pleasing to God, which is your rational (logical, intelligent) act of worship. And be not conformed to this world [any longer with its superficial values and customs] but be transformed and progressively changed [as you mature spiritually] by the renewing of your mind [focusing on godly values and ethical attitudes], so that you may prove [for yourselves] what the will of God is, that which is good and acceptable and perfect [in His plan and purpose for you]."* (Romans 12:1-2 AMP).

All things work together for the good when you are in Jesus; and there is so much power in the fact that the enemy tried you but he didn't succeed. If the enemy never attack your mind, how can you truthfully say that you have the mind of Christ. You can only testify about things that you have experienced and your progress in the kingdom can only be measured by your victories in the spirit. It is important that you know the tactics of the enemy. It is even more important that you know that God has given you power and authority over all the attempts of the enemy. Keep in mind that you are always dealing with a defeated enemy that works with a persistent effort to destroy your Christ aligned mind.

Shelia R. Pearson

From My Heart to Yours

It is my prayer that once you hear the voice of God, immediate obedience will kick in and you will forever enjoy the benefits of moving with the voice of God. It is time to hear God and to allow Him and Him alone to orchestrate your steps. The Lord is instructing you to hear His voice because He opens His lips to give you priceless things. It is His desire that you listen to His instructions with an attitude of keeping His ways. You can't ever go wrong taking the steps that God has given you to take. Obeying God in doing ministry the way He has ordained you to do it will give you the peace you've only dreamed of having. It is through this level of maturity that you gain God's favor and are rewarded with an outpouring of His blessings. So it is my prayer that you learn to move synchronized with the Spirit of God and that nothing will keep you from enjoying the promises that He has designed just for you.

CHAPTER 6

The Power of Love

Your weaknesses are tried so that God can be glorified. When the enemy manifests his best work, God is still in control. Once you have given yourselves to the truth of the Word, you are also empowered to live the Word. This is where your dependence in God and God alone comes in. It is your job to maintain focus because He is the One who strengthens you. He is the God that created the waster to destroy. God actually uses the enemy to make you better. This truth reminds me of the Word given to the Apostle Paul during a stressful moment. Paul explains, *"Because of the surpassing greatness and extraordinary nature of the revelations [which I received from God], for this reason, to keep me from thinking of myself as important, a thorn in the flesh was given to me, a messenger of Satan, to torment and harass me—to keep me from exalting myself! Concerning this I pleaded with the Lord three times that it might leave me; but He has said to me, 'My grace is sufficient for you [My lovingkindness and My mercy are more than enough—always available—regardless of the situation]; for [My] power is being perfected [and is completed and shows itself most effectively] in [your] weakness.' Therefore, I will all the more gladly boast in my weaknesses, so that the power of Christ [may completely enfold me and] may dwell in me. So I am well pleased with weaknesses, with insults, with distresses, with persecutions, and with difficulties, for the sake of Christ; for when I am weak [in human strength], then I am strong [truly able, truly powerful, truly drawing from God's strength]."* (2 Corinthians 12:7-10 AMP).

Every spirit filled believer should find themselves in the same mindset illustrated by the Apostle Paul. During testing times you shouldn't be given over to the test. You should only be drawing your strength from

God with a focused mind, knowing that in your insufficiencies God is ready to show you that His grace is sufficient. Know that He will always lift that standard for you but you must always present the whole of yourselves to Him. A dedication to Him that will never allow the filtrations of the enemy to manifest in your lives. The enemy will always try you but God must always have complete and total control.

The enemy's main target is our love walk because love is one of the greatest gifts given to man. Satan understands that we serve a God of love and we can only demonstrate Him through our acts of love. He also knows that if he could convince us to act contrary, he can completely leer us off the path of righteousness. Coming short in this expression is not part of God's plan. He empowered us to work great exploits for His kingdom and this is impossible if we fail to display His character. God has given us eyes to see and it is vital that we see properly.

Division is another tactic the enemy uses to target our love walk. This work of the enemy has no power, but this is how he manifests his best work in the church. It is his desire to divide and conquer. The enemy understands that once we begin going after titles and denominations, the love walk turns into a walk of competition. This too is not the plan of God. He has anointed us to be knitted together and by all means necessary we must function as one body in Christ.

Love and Unity

It is God's love for His creation that births out the spirit of intercession. There is no divide in this work of the spirit. Love and unity must be the focal point and it is important that we become balanced in these areas. God is waiting on the saints to come together in the power of truly demonstrating Him. Take note of Ephesians 3:18 AMP; it states, *"That you may have the power and be strong to apprehend and grasp **with all the saints** [God's devoted people, the experience of that love] what is the breadth and length and height and depth [of it]; [that you may really come] to know [practically, through experience for yourselves] the love of Christ, which far surpasses mere knowledge [without experience]; that you may be filled [through all your being] unto all the fullness of God [may have the richest measure of the divine Presence, and become a body wholly filled and flooded with God Himself]!"* This Word is simply highlighting the importance of love and unity. We must be delivered from thinking that God is shining a special glory on our church or denomination alone. I am addressing this because I have encountered witnesses that believe that God has specifically chose their denomination as the chosen bride. This is one of the greatest deceptions of Satan. God is looking for a moment in time where He can fill His whole body of believers with the richest measure of His divine Presence. Jesus is the Great Intercessor and He became sin to deliver humanity. He did not become an Advocate for no particular denomination, gift, race or gender.

One of the worse divides we find in the body of Christ is through leadership. This is going on in the church rather we admit to this truth or not. The key thing we must understand as leaders is that God desires to fill all things with Himself. *"He Who descended is the [very] same as He who also has ascended high above all the heavens, that He [His presence] might fill all things (the whole universe, from the lowest to the highest)."* (Ephesians 4:10 AMP). Notice that God didn't discriminate, it is His desire to make a difference in the entire universe. All of the gifts in the body are meant to work in harmony with one another. The Bible teaches us that the gifts were *"[varied; He Himself appointed and gave men to us] some to be apostles (special messengers), some prophets (inspired preachers and expounders), some evangelists (preachers of the Gospel, traveling missionaries), some pastors (shepherds of His flock) and teachers."* (Ephesians 4:11AMP). Notice that God empowered five distinct gifts to edify the church and know that He expect all five to function according to His perfect will.

In order to birth out a fully developed church, we must do things God's way. God gave His gifts to the body to perfect and fully equip the saints to minister toward building up the church (Ephesians 4:12-13). These instructions were not given to the pastor alone and it is vital that we as the gifts in the body start truly demonstrating oneness with power. It is heart wrenching how we have allowed the gifts that God has set in place to build and edify to become such a divided demonstration in the church today. Once we learn to do things according to the Word of God, we will have a very strong and stable foundation. We will also attain the oneness of faith that God is patiently waiting on us to manifest in this hour.

This word is clearly putting a spotlight on the enemy. The sad part about this truth is that he is doing his best work in the church. I know that some leaders will still argue the fact that they are anointed to demonstrate all five gifts. They have convinced themselves that their church will continue to grow in the capacity ordained for it to grow even if they never put the gifts in the body to work. It is best that we trust, believe and apply the Word that has been given to us. As leaders we want God to reward us for our good works, but only the ones who are lowly in spirit will obtain honor (Proverbs 29:23). The enemy thrives on pride, but humility is powerful and it has a way of ridding us of our haughty ways. It is time we humble ourselves enough to be obedient to *all* of the Word. The doctrine of man will never elevate us in the spirit. It is God's way or no way!

Shelia R. Pearson
From My Heart to Yours

It is my prayer that as you hear my heart you understand God's heart. God has given us His Spirit to truly represent Him and it starts with functioning as one body in Christ. The enemy gains so much ground in the lives of believers through the tainted spirit of division. It is my prayer that you would connect with me to destroy the works of Satan. I pray that he would battle with us only to lose because of the power of the love of God that operates through our lives daily. This is God's holy intent for His creation and I pray that you would help me spread this message of love and unity in Jesus name.

Advancing for Kingdom Sake!

Chapter 7

The Fear of Rejection

God's growth process places a command on us to learn endurance. There is no way of seeing what is at the end of the road if we allow the trials at the middle of the road to stop us. The Bible teaches us that we should rejoice whenever test and trials present themselves. We are encouraged to, *"Let endurance and steadfastness and patience have full play and do a thorough work so that we may be [people] perfectly and fully developed [with no defects], lacking in nothing."* (James 1:4 AMP). We are to hold on to every promise regardless of the things sent to break our focus. If God allowed a test to present itself, it is only part of the plan. Every struggle has a way of equipping us for the rest of the journey.

In Chapter 5 I mentioned my season of running from the church even though I was called to the church. I convinced myself that God was okay with me traveling from place to place if the leaders didn't know how to treat me. This was not the will of God for my life because it was impossible for me to continue the growth process if I didn't remain planted. Jesus explains it this way, *"Those along the traveled road are the people who have heard the word; then the devil comes and carries away the message out of their hearts, that they may not believe (acknowledge Me as their Savior and devote themselves to Me) and be saved [here and hereafter]. And those upon the rock [are the people] who, when they hear [the Word], receive and welcome it with joy, but these have no root. They believe for a while, and in time of trial and temptation fall away (withdraw and stand aloof). And as for what fell among the thorns, these are [the people] who hear, but as they go on their way they are choked and suffocated with anxieties and cares and riches and pleasures of life, and their fruit does not ripen (come to maturity and perfection)."* (Luke 8:12-

14 AMP). An image is being demonstrated about the seriousness of being rooted and grounded in the proper places. We will only see the manifestations of the promises of God if we plant ourselves in our ordained places to grow. Once God has given us our heavenly instructions, it is best that we obey immediately. Why hinder our growth process if God has given us all we need to continue advancing in His kingdom?

This brings to mind the season I allowed the enemy to gain a foothold in my life. During this time I was instructed to relocate to my hometown to start my prayer ministry. After sharing my vision with a select few the warfare began. Once leaders failed to comply, I began pulling on intercessors within the local churches. This approach caused my warfare to intensify because certain leaders viewed me as someone that was scattering their sheep. I was rejected on extreme levels and my call to prayer intercession in my hometown was viewed as failure.

After experiencing this great disappointment, I returned to Memphis, TN. The pain of this experience turned my heart completely away from leadership. It caused me to guard my heart with all diligence. It was hard for me to start fresh in any church because I didn't trust anyone, especially leaders. The old had wrapped itself around me like a protected garment and it was difficult to remain planted.

During this season, God allowed me to meet my spiritual mother, Prophetess Jessica Selvy-Davis. It was truly a blessing to meet my Kingdom Seekers Ministry of the Arts family. My life was truly realigned through the truth that was revealed through Prophetess Jessica. Through her prophetic release I was able to see how I had allowed the fear of rejection to stagnate me in ministry. The rejection that I experienced in my hometown placed me in a spiritual prison. The unholy actions from leaders caused me to build my own prison walls. God was not pleased with these actions and He continued dealing with my heart by using my Kingdom Seekers family. I will never forget God using my sister Prophetess Joni Selvy-Brown to correct me. She walked up to me and said I hear the Lord saying, *"Do it again, do it again, do it again."* She also stated, *"God said He never told you to stop!"* I knew exactly what the Lord was saying because during this time my heart had turned completely away from leadership and so had my prayers.

The instructions were very clear but I wrestled with what I knew the Lord was speaking to me in that season. God never stopped dealing with me about my heart condition towards leaders. I will never forget receiving a call from an old friend. He opened up the conversation by ministering to me about Jonah and how his disobedience landed him in the belly of the fish. My old friend had no idea that God was using him to redirect my total life. As I continued to make detours, I kept ending up on dead end roads. It was so important that I recognized the spirits that was trying to rob me of my success story. We all have stories to tell and it is vital that we recognize the strongholds that are hindering us from walking in the right direction. We must continue fighting the enemy of the mind because he is a persistent dream killer. He never lets up when it comes to diminishing our faith. He understands that fear is powerful enough to rob us of our demonstrations of faith.

God began explaining how important it was that I didn't neglect the gift that was within me. He commanded me to embrace 1 Timothy 4:14-16 AMP; it states, *"Do not neglect the spiritual gift within you, [that special endowment] which was intentionally bestowed to you [by the Holy Spirit] through prophetic utterance when the elders laid their hands on you [at your ordination]. Practice and work hard on these things; be absorbed in them [completely occupied in your ministry], so that your progress will be evident to all. Pay close attention to yourself [concentrate on your personal development] and your teaching; persevere in these things [hold to them], for as you do this you will ensure salvation both for yourself and for those who hear you."*

After receiving this Word from the Lord, I knew that it would be impossible to be completely occupied in my ministry if I didn't get my heart right towards the people that I was called to cover in the spirit. He was placing a command on me to stop pretending to be blind to truth. Getting on the right path and staying on the right path had to become my pursuit. The Bible in 1 Corinthians 2:9 teaches us, *"Eye has not seen and ear has not heard and has not entered into the heart of man, [all that] God has prepared (make and keeps ready) for those who love [who hold Him in affectionate reverence, promptly obeying Him and gratefully recognizing the benefits He have bestowed]."* Once I understood the seriousness of obeying all of God's instructions, I realigned myself in the spirit with an attitude of staying planted. I also began paying close attention to myself, my personal development, and my teaching just as the Word of God had instructed me to do. Through this act of obedience, many doors opened wide unto me. Once God speaks and you take on an ear to hear, it is vital that your hearing leads you into immediate obedience. God does not want us to be ready listeners with no works to show for it. Through my obedience the windows of heaven opened wide unto me and God literally overflowed me with more than enough.

Shelia R. Pearson

Executing Dream Killers

It is our job to recognize the things in our lives that need to take flight. Fear is one of the enemies that we must cast down the minute we realize that he has manifested in our lives. The moment the Lord used my spiritual mother to identify the fear of rejection, I should have dealt with that spirit and obeyed the voice of God. I allowed his power over me to dominate. Fear operates with enough power to rob us of our true identity. It has enough trickery to stagnate us, leaving us in a place of defeat. Fear paints images of nothing but death because it comes with goals in mind and those goals are aimed towards stealing, killing, and destroying. It is a silent killer and if we never detect that it is there, it slowly takes us out. We find ourselves giving excuse after excuse as to why we're not obeying God. I can help God's people recognize this spirit only because of the grip it once had on my life. Fear must be given access to your domain and when it enters, it works at a steady pace to abort your destiny. The enemy does not waste time with people who do not have goals in mind. His focus is on instruments with dreams and passions to do kingdom works. People who are purpose driven are extremely hated by the enemy because of their demonstrations of faith.

The promises of God must always be magnified greater than the tactics of the enemy. It is so important that we maintain our confessions of faith when our dream killers began manifesting themselves. Yes, doubt and fear come with a plan to abort destiny. They show up in our lives with hope to shift our standing posture; but the enemy understands that faith puts a driving force within us. It puts a determination within us that displays victory regardless of what he sends our way.

The Word of God questions us about our demonstrations of faith. It states, *"What is the use (profit), my brethren, for anyone to profess to have faith if he has no [good] works [to show for it]? Can [such faith save his soul]?"* (James 2:14). Faith is not mere words being released, but it comes with demonstrations of God's power. It has no room for doubt because it is too busy making things happen for the kingdom of God. *The Bible explains it this way, "So also faith if it does not have works (deeds and actions of obedience to back it up, by itself is destitute of power (inoperative dead)."* (James 2:14 AMP). God supplies power to see true manifestations in the earth realm and we must understand that we are empowered to not just have faith but to operate in faith.

Progress is all that God expects of us. He is looking for a steady momentum that refuse to be side-tracked by doubt and fear. We must walk as true ambassadors for God. He has given us His Word to demolish all dream killers. Once we recognize these violating spirits, it is our duty as soldiers to deal with them with the arsenal that God has supplied. God has given us the spirit of power, love, and a well-balanced mind and that is all that He expects to see manifesting in our lives during testing times.

Shelia R. Pearson

From My Heart to Yours

God's instructions are the only instructions you need for life. It is vital that you maintain your stand in Him. You have a real enemy to fight and know that it is the job of Satan to work against God's preordained plan for your life. The Lord makes no mistakes and His instructions will only manifest greatness in your life. Stay rooted and grounded in truth and refuse to allow doubt and fear to stagnate you in the spirit. God is in the business of giving you a good future but know that you must make the decision to stay on your road to success.

Chapter 8
Dethroning Satan

We must always stand on the fact that our wrestle is never with physical opponents (1 Corinthians 10:4). The enemy will always stir up things for our natural eyes to see. It is his desire that we fail at truly demonstrating the dominion that God has given us. So, he finds joy in us wasting time fighting natural battles; but God has empowered us to win. He has given us all that we need to live victoriously as a Christian.

The season I wrestled with my flesh I found security in the Word of God. I had to remind myself that a renewal had taken place in my life and that the old was no longer welcomed. Our minds must learn to reject sin because the wrestle is always in our thinking. Our victorious living starts and is maintained once we learn to restrain our flesh. This flesh and the desires of it died when we were baptized into Christ's death. We were buried, therefore *"with Him by the baptism into death, so that just as Christ was raised from the dead by the glorious [power] of the Father, so we too might [habitually] live and behave in newness of life."* (Romans 6:3-4 AMP). This truth of the Word belongs to us and we must use it as our weapon of defense during trying times.

Satan is the prime promoter of sin and he desire total control. The Bible encourages us to *"Let not sin therefore rule as king in our (short-lived, perishable) bodies to make us yield to its cravings and be subject to its lusts and evil passions."* (Romans 6:12 AMPC). This Word is painting a true image of Satan and we must see truth about him to really deal with him. It is his desire to rule in our lives as king. A king has the right to rule completely and totally with no need for approval from any representative body. This level of authority for a king has been set in order by God. The thing about Satan, he is violating on territory that he has no rights to and we are empowered to dethrone him. We must release the power of the Word and dislodge him from the seats he has established in our lives.

Keep the Distracting Doors Closed!

"For no temptation (no trial regarded as enticing to sin), [no matter how it comes or where it leads] has overtaken you and laid hold on you that is not common to man [that is, no temptation or trial has come to you that is beyond human resistance and that is not adjusted and adapted and belonging to human experience, and such as man can bear]. But God is faithful [to His Word and to His compassionate nature], and He [can be trusted] not to let you be tempted and tried and assayed beyond your ability and strength of resistance and power to endure, but with the temptation He will [always] also provide the way out (the means of escape to a landing place), that you may be capable and strong and powerful to bear up under it patiently." (1Corinthians 10:13 AMP). God has already given us a way out of every enticing attack, so we must abort all the excuses we make to remain in sin. The enemy will stay on his job as tempter and accuser and it is important that we recognize him and function in our power to resist him.

The enemy uses tactics to break our focused minds. His distractions are meant to take us off our preordained course. He brings mental confusion and works with great persistence to turn a stable mind into a wavering one. There is no way to focus our attention on the things that matter when we are given over to a distracting spirit. As believers we must keep in mind that we have an enemy that is always working to get us off the course of action that God has given us. The Word encourages us to maintain a focused mind; it states, *"Be well balanced (temperate, sober of mind) be vigilant and cautious at all times; for that enemy of yours, the devil, roams around like a lion roaring [in fierce hunger] seeking someone to seize upon and devour. Withstand him; be firm in faith [against his onset-rooted, established, strong, immovable, and determined], knowing that the same (identical sufferings are appointed to your brotherhood (the whole body of Christians) throughout the world."* (1 Peter 5:8-9 AMPC). The enemy will always work against our standing abilities but we must always use God's equipping power to maintain our stand in the spirit. Once God makes His instructions clear, it is up to us to fight to stay on course. By all means necessary we must stay on the path that leads to our divine destiny. We must maintain a Christ aligned mind by *"casting down vain imaginations, and every high thing that exalts itself against the knowledge of God and bringing into captivity every thought to the obedience of Christ."* (2 Corinthians 10:3-5 AMP). We can't allow our minds to have free course and sometimes we will have to fight a little harder to maintain our stand. The most rewarding thing about this wrestle in the spirit is the fact that we've been given the weaponry we need to counteract all of the enemy's attacks.

Shelia R. Pearson

From My Heart to Yours

Throughout the Bible we have been informed that God has given us all we need to live over-coming Christian lives. I am convinced that God is not going to do what He has equipped us to do. We have been given instructions to make preparation for our enemy. He tells us to be strong in the Lord and in the power of His might. We have also been instructed to draw our strength from Him, to stand and to put on the whole armor of God. Our victory starts with using everything that God has given us. We must armor ourselves with the Word of God, using it as our offensive and defensive weapon. It is my prayer that you, as believer, begin operating in the power and authority given to you and that you will walk in the victory that was established for you before the foundation of the world.

Advancing for Kingdom Sake!

CHAPTER 9
Enough is Enough!

God is speaking loud and clear that enough is enough! He's dealing with the contrary in this season and He expects us as believers to deal with the enemy on every level. He should not have advantage in the house of God and we are called to see and deal with every manifestation. Now Satan has become very crafty with his plans. He understands that the growth process is hindered when God's Word becomes contaminated with the wisdom of man. Attending church services is not good enough because through the craftiness of Satan the true Word has been snatched from the mouths of some of our leaders. False doctrine is having free course due to God's people failing to gain a personal relationship with Christ. The devil is totally aware of our confidence in man and he is organizing his best work through leadership. He does not mind us embracing this one question, *"And how are they to hear without a preacher?"* (Romans 10:14). It is important that we don't stop at this one question. In the next verse another valuable question is ask, *"And how can men [be expected to] preach unless they are sent?"* (Romans 10:15).

The Word of God paints an image of the contrary; it states, *"For there are many disorderly and unruly men who are idle (vain, empty) misleading talkers and self-deceivers and deceivers of others. [This is true] especially of those of the circumcision party. Their mouths must be stopped, for they are mentally distressing and subverting whole families by teaching what they ought not to teach, for the purpose of getting base advantage and disreputable gain."* (Titus 1: 10-11 AMP). Some leaders are coming dressed as shepherds but under the surface they are wolves. They are weakening the body through their own man-made doctrine and we must become more aware. It is important that we rightly discern the heart condition of leaders.

Apostle Paul tells us to *"Study and be eager and do our utmost to present ourselves to God approved (tested by trial), workmen who has no cause to be ashamed, correctly analyzing and accurately dividing [rightly handling and skillfully teaching] the Word of Truth. But avoid empty (vain, useless, idle) talk, for it will lead people into more and more ungodliness. And their teaching [will devour; it] will eat its way like cancer or spread like gangrene."* (2 Timothy 2:15 AMP). If we fail to study the Word of God for ourselves, we will be open to the deception of Satan. It does not matter how much we gather to hear the Word - we must be found faithful to God on a personal level.

God is waiting on us to seek for His wisdom and not the wisdom of man. Growing closer to God gives us the eyes to see truth and the ability to separate ourselves from the contrary. Once we learn to separate ourselves from ungodly things, God will give us His power in abundant measures. Apostle Paul explains it this way, *"So whoever cleanses himself [from what is ignoble and unclean, who separates himself from contact with contaminating and corrupting influences] will [then himself] be a vessel set apart and useful for honorable and noble purposes consecrated and profitable to the Master, fit and ready for any good work."* (2 Timothy 2:21 AMP).

Recognizing Deceivers

"They have eyes full of harlotry, insatiable for sin. They beguile and bait and lure away unstable souls. Their hearts are trained in covetousness (lust, greed), [they are] children of a curse [exposed to cursing]." (2 Peter 2:14 AMP).

I went through a season where I held on to the form. I allowed a form of godliness to operate consistently in my life and I grew accustomed to it. I found myself becoming desensitized to the truth and I was opened to the deception of Satan. It wasn't until I obeyed God in turning away from false representatives that I began seeing the manifestation of the promise. I had dealt with the work of Satan operating through leadership for years. When I relocated from my hometown to Memphis, TN for a season of rest, God used this time to show me how immature I was in the faith. I had been damaged in marriage and ministry and was very weak when it came to obeying all of God's instructions. While I was being weighed down by the burden of my trials, God uncovered a contrary spirit in the pulpit. I joined a ministry that was shepherded by a single man. During this time, I was in a posture of weakness when it came to my ministry and marriage - so, holding on to either one had become a thing of the past.

God instructed me to remain faithful to what He had given me regardless of what I had to suffer; but through my weakened state, deceiving words from the mouth of my newly found leader began guiding me. I completely stopped doing my prayer gatherings and started preaching on a regular basis at my new church. My vision was being ignored as I continued to embrace the newness I had stepped into. Within months of serving, my pastor started making advances towards me as if I was single and available. He went as far as offering me money to move into my own apartment. He was very persuasive and due to past hurts, I found myself moments away from aborting the promises concerning my marriage and ministry. I know that I experienced 2 Timothy 3:6-8 AMP only that I may have enough experience to warn the body of Christ. I know that I can cry with a loud voice proclaiming that the spirit of apostacy is still at work in the church. God is placing a command on us to recognize and turn away from the *forms* that are surfacing in the house of God. *"For among them are those who worm their way into homes and captivate silly weak-natured and spiritually dwarfed women."* (2 Timothy 3:6 AMP). Through my weak and immature nature, a leader's words beguiled me. I was in a state of confusion and pain, so therefore, I opened myself up for contamination. The Word states that, *"These weak women will listen to anybody who will teach them; they are forever inquiring and getting information but are never able to arrive at a recognition and knowledge of the Truth. Now just as Jannes and Jambres were hostile to and resisted Moses, so these men also are hostile to and oppose the Truth. They have depraved and distorted minds and are reprobate and counterfeit and to rejected as far as the faith is concerned."* (2 Timothy 3:7-8 AMP).

Through my wounded heart the enemy rushed in to abort God's plans for my life. He used a man dressed as a shepherd of God's flock, someone betraying to be a true representative of God. The enemy chose a man that was called to point me in the right direction. I can proudly say that regardless of how close the enemy came to destroying God's plans for my marriage and ministry, he did not succeed! God is removing blinders off of the eyes of the believers, giving us eyes to detect the wickedness of Satan. A spotlight is on the craftiness that is trying to creep into God's house to destroy the true representatives. The Word promised that these individuals will not make it very far in their attempts; it states, *"But they will not get very far, for their rash folly will become obvious to everybody, as was that of those [magicians mentioned]."* (2 Timothy 3:9 AMP).

This is still going on in the house of God in this day and time. I am a witness that it is real and I am a voice releasing the truth into the hearts of every believer that is humble enough to receive. Enough is enough, these are the words that God is speaking in this hour. Judgment is coming to the house of God and it is time to repent. I know that every false representative is aware of their folly and as a voice in this earth realm I cry, *"REPENT NOW!"*

Shelia R. Pearson
From My Heart to Yours

As a leader, God has made me very transparent and I am grateful. It is actually a blessing to minister through my life's experiences. I know that if the enemy was bold enough to try me during my immature stage, I am sure he's bold enough to try you and anybody connected to you. It is my prayer that you see him regardless of how he chooses to manifest. If we don't expose him, he will continue to gain ground in the house that is designed to carry the glory of God. It is my prayer that God would give you the ability to see and deal with the enemy on every level. There are so many false representatives having their way in the church and this must stop! It is my prayer that you refuse to allow anything to silence you. I also pray that you would be very bold in the spirit once the tempter decides to make his bold appearance.

Advancing for Kingdom Sake!

Shelia R. Pearson

CHAPTER 10
Taking Your Exalted Seat

God has made us to sit down in heavenly places with Him. Through His life, death, and resurrection we have been given access to an exalted seat. Once we take this seat, a transfiguration takes place in the supernatural realm. We are given the power and authority to function strictly in the spirit. This power identifies us as children of the living God. It also shifts us into a higher level of faith, empowering us to view ourselves through the eyes of God. The Bible teaches us that *"When we were dead (slain) by [our own] shortcomings and trespasses, he made us alive together in fellowship and in union with Christ; [He gave us the very life with which He quickened Him, for] it is by grace (His favor and mercy which you did not deserve) that you are saved (delivered from judgement and made partakers of Christ's salvation). And He raised us up together with Him and made us sit down together [giving joint seating with Him] in the heavenly sphere [by virtue of our being] in Christ Jesus (the Messiah, the Anointed One)."* (Ephesians 2:5-6 AMP).

The key thing to understand is that this truth does not automatically stop the enemy's attempts. It is the job of Satan to keep us living in the carnal nature or dictated by our fleshy desires. But once we are seated in the heavenlies we are translated into a new kingdom. An introduction takes place in our lives that presents new authority, new power and a supernatural rank in the spirit. This new kingdom gives us power and authority over Satan. Colossians 1:13 AMP explains it this way, *"[The Father] has delivered and drawn us to Himself out of the control and dominion of darkness and has transferred us into the kingdom of the Son of His love."* Taking this seat shifts us into a state of being governed by the Spirit of God. Once we are seated, *"We are in Him, made full and having come to fullness of life [in Christ, we too are filled with the Godhead—Father, Son and Holy Spirit—and reach a full spiritual stature]. And He is the Head of all rule and authority [of every angelic principality and power]. In Him also we were circumcised with a circumcision not made with hands, but in a [spiritual] circumcision [performed by] Christ by stripping off the body of the flesh (the whole corrupt, carnal nature with its passions and lusts)."* (Colossians 2:10-11 AMP).

Taking this seat elevates us into a life lived in the spirit and it frees us from the world's way of thinking. We are translated into a kingdom that is designed for the set apart ones. God places a seal of ownership upon us that grants us a spiritual inheritance. We become a royal family and all the benefits of heaven belong to us. It is a privilege to be seated in heavenly places; a seat in which we did not deserve but inherited by being connected to the Savior. Once we took a seat in Christ, we became overcomers. He gave us the supernatural ability to overcome every manifested attack. Yes, the enemy is known to steal, kill and destroy but our focus should remain on the fact that Christ came to give us life and life more abundantly. The victory in the cross destroyed the works of the devil. *"[God] disarmed the principalities and powers that were ranged against us and made a bold display and public example of them, in triumphing over them in Him and in it [the cross]."* (Colossians 2:15 AMP). It is our job to continue displaying the victory that we have in this exalted seat. It does not matter how the enemy makes himself known - God should always be magnified greater than our enemy.

Redeeming the Time!

Now that we have taken our exalted seat, we should no longer let sin rule as king in our bodies. It is our job to fight against the cravings and lust of the flesh (Romans 6:12 AMP). If we fail to resist the worldly tendencies, we will also fail at being recognized as Christians. It is vital that we understand that if we are not Christ-like, we will not be accepted by Him. The Bible teaches us, *"So then those who are living the life of the flesh [catering to the appetites and impulses of their carnal nature] cannot please or satisfy God or be accepted by Him."* (Romans 8:8 AMP). Once we take this seat in Christ, we must live the life. Time is out when it comes to thinking that accepting Christ is all we need to do.

The Word has been given to us so that we can learn and live the life of Christ. We are taught that the Word of God must be on our lips and in our hearts. It goes on to let us know that embracing the Word is our basis and should be the object of faith in which we preach (Romans 10:8-10 AMP). The Word of God must be given free course to reconstruct our thinking. If we open our hearts to receive the Word, it will supernaturally separate us from the world. It will give us the ability to function as true representatives of Christ. Time is out when it comes to thinking that we can do any and everything we are bold enough to do. God will gladly reward us for the deeds we've done in our bodies. He will not ignore the contrary things just because we verbally confessed that we believed He died for our sins. If we believe He died for our sins, why do we continue sinning? He died that we may have the power to demonstrate and imitate

Him. He filled us with His Spirit for the purpose of delivering us from the wages of sin (Romans 6:23 AMP).

Time is out when it comes to watering down the true message of salvation. If we are truly the children of God, the flesh shouldn't be dominating in our lives. The Word teaches us that, *"If we live according to [the dictates of] the flesh, we will surly die. But if through the power of the [Holy] Spirit we are [habitually] putting to death (making extinct, deadening) the [evil] deeds prompted by the body, we shall [really and genuinely] live forever."* (Romans 8:13 AMP)! It is time to live the life we are preaching about. We must put our lives in perspective and command our bodies and souls to line up with the things of the Spirit.

Giving ourselves to the things of the Spirit requires us taking our eyes off of our surroundings. Those things that occur for our natural eyes to see are usually the things that get us off of God's preordained course. Maintaining a spiritual mindset requires us to be discipline in the study of the Word. Learning the Word equips us for the many pressure tactics of the enemy. We are encouraged to, *"Study and be eager and do our utmost to present ourselves to God approved (tested by trial), workmen who has no cause to be ashamed, correctly analyzing and accurately dividing [rightly handling and skillfully teaching] the Word of Truth. But avoid empty (vain, useless, idle) talk, for it will lead people into more and more ungodliness. And their teaching [will devour; it] will eat its way like cancer or spread like gangrene."* (2 Timothy 2:15 AMP). It is time that we study the Word long enough and strong enough to apply it to our lives daily.

From My Heart to Yours

    I am declaring that time is out for playing with the power that God has made available. If you are aware of the righteous path, it is best to remain on your road to success. If you know the right way, it is time to do it the right way. God has given you power to live according to His standards and it is time you access that power. Why continue walking in the wrong direction when you know you can only receive the wrong results? Wisdom is screaming out and it is my prayer that you take heed to the voice of God. It is my prayer that you no longer waste time with God's precious time.

Shelia R. Pearson

Chapter 11

Blazing a Trail of Righteousness

An examination is needed when it comes to walking in the fullness of who we are. It is important that we function in the spirit according to the power given to us. Once I started questioning God concerning the anointing He had placed on my life, it was obvious that I wasn't using His power adequately. I had to embrace the fact when much is given, much is required. God did not come slack when it came to the outpouring of His Spirit but I was only experiencing this power in silence. This was not the will of God for my life and know that it is not the will of God for yours either. Intercessors are given the ability to see things that most people can't see. So, God made it clear that I was called to the body of Christ and I was also empowered to deal with every exalted seat of Satan.

He spoke, *"I have anointed you to blaze a trail of righteousness!"* God was commanding me to get out of my comfort zone and to do ministry the way He had empowered me to do it. One thing we can say about a blaze is that it is impossible to go unnoticed. God has given intercessors the power to decree and declare things in the Earth. Once we learn to obey God, we will see great manifestations of His power. He will quickly bring things to past right before our eyes. God uncovers and reveals truth so that we can get busy making things happen. He is totally aware of the assignments He has given to each of us and we will be held accountable. It is time that we embrace the fact that obedience is better than sacrifice. If God has given us instructions, they were given for the edification of His kingdoms. Some of the definitions given for the word "blaze" in the Merriam-Webster's Dictionary are "intensely burning fire," "active burn," and "sudden bursting forth of flames."

All of these definitions are great but the ones that stands out the most are "an intense direct light "and to "mark (a trail) with blazes." I declare that this is the posture of every called-out intercessor. They are on fire for God and everything contrary to God is being utterly destroyed. They are opening their mouths to deal with every exalted seat of Satan. I release this declaration with all the power and authority given to me. It is time that the fire carriers get to work and those pretending to be fire carriers to take heed. There is no way of destroying the works of Satan if we are his best employees. God is opening the mouths of the chosen and He is orchestrating their steps. No longer will there be silence in the land.

God's chosen people are embracing the fact that they are empowered to work great exploits. Voices are being raised in this season to tear down strongholds. The consuming fire of God is being released to burn down all satanic altars. I am releasing this in obedience and if you are reading this, it is time that you examine your heart. God is not playing with us; it is either complete obedience or no obedience. We must stabilize ourselves in the seat that God has given us. Obedience must become the lifestyle of the believer; and know that we cannot partially obey God because He did not partially fill us with Himself. We are the vessels God chose to work through and we must maintain our stand as true examples of righteousness. God saved us, filled us, and sanctified us holy for kingdom purposes. Our lives must become the light that direct others to the path of righteousness. Notice in the beginning God separated the darkness from the light and He acknowledged that the light was good.

Shelia R. Pearson

Throughout the Bible the righteous people of God were commanded to not just focus on the light but to walk in the light. In 1 Thessalonians 5:5 KJV we are taught that, *"We are children of light, children of the day. We are not of the night or of the darkness."* A foundation was laid in the beginning of creation and a separation took place that was meant to be followed. As we enter into a life of intercession, it is vital that we embrace the seriousness of being distinguished for the Lord. This will take us truly representing the One who sanctified us holy. Just as He is Light, we must become the light that separate ourselves from darkness. Jesus spoke saying, *"I am the light of the world. Whoever follows me will not walk in the darkness but will have the light."* (John 8:18 KJV).

It should be understood, if Jesus is represented as light, the devil must be behind the wicked and twisted manifestations in the world today. This truth really can't be simplified any greater than this and it may be even viewed as elementary. But, regardless of how this Word is received, it is a truth that must be enforced again and again. The Word teaches us that judgement is coming to those who pretend to be blind to the truth. It states, *"Woe unto them that call evil good, and good evil; that put darkness for light, and light for darkness; that put bitter for sweet, and sweet for bitter."* (Isaiah 5:50 KJV). This is a message for all who continue to play with God's righteous Law.

It does not matter who you are in the eyes of man, God is a god who is fully capable of seeing all things and He will judge all things. Sin does not go unnoticed; the deeds of unrighteousness do not go unpunished. Every soul will have to stand before God and He will judge each of us righteously. We have entered into a time where the ways of the world are taking high and exalted seats. This is taking place even in the houses claiming to be anointed for God's holy presence. It is best that we recognize that God is truly holy and that He refuses to dwell in unclean temples. It may appear to some that judgment will never manifest itself; but there is a time and a season for every purpose under the sun. *"So do not make hasty or premature judgements before the time when the Lord comes [again], for He will both bring to light the secret things that are [now hidden] in darkness and disclose and expose the [secret] aims (motives and purposes) of hearts. Then every man will receive his [due] commendation from God."* (1 Corinthians 4:5 AMP). I am delighted to know that God will not look at the church I attended or the blood lineage I was born into. It is a blessing to know that God will judge each one of us and this speaks volumes to how special we are on individual levels.

God took His time to uniquely create all of us and He gave us special designs and specific instructions. There is no room to accuse anyone for our shortcomings in life. God presented Himself as light to all and it is totally up to us if we choose to walk after the Light. We serve a just God and He will never force His righteous Law upon us. Yes, He uses anointed vessels to enforce His righteous way but we are all given a choice. We will be judged according to the walk we decided to take. The Bible encourages us to walk in newness of life. We are reminded that we were once darkness, but now we are light in the Lord. This Word encourages us to *walk as children of Light [live as those who are native-born to the Light] (for the fruit [the effect the result] of the light consist in all goodness and righteousness and truth), try to learn [by experience] what is pleasing to the Lord [and let your lifestyle be examples of what is most acceptable to Him—your behavior expressing gratitude to God for your salvation]. Do not participate in the worthless and unproductive deeds of darkness, but instead expose them [by exemplifying personal integrity, moral courage, and godly character]; for it is disgraceful even to mention the things that such people practice in secret. But all things become visible when they are exposed by the light [of God's precepts], for it is light that makes everything visible. For this reason He says, 'Awake O sleeper, and arise from the dead, And Christ will shine [as dawn] upon you and give you light. Therefore see that you walk carefully [living life with honor, purpose, and courage, shunning those who tolerate and enable evil], not as the unwise, but as wise [sensible, intelligent, discerning people], making the very most of your time [on earth, recognizing and taking advantage of each opportunity and using it with wisdom and diligence], because the days are [filled with] evil. Therefore do not be foolish and thoughtless but understand and firmly grasp what the will of the Lord is."* (Ephesians 5:8-17 AMP).

    The will of the Lord is proclaimed clearly that we are to walk in the light! We are to display all that God created us to be. It is obvious that God wanted us to walk as duplicates of Him. If this wasn't so, he wouldn't have created us in His very image. The fact that God created mankind as images of Himself, we are to present all that He is to everyone we meet. Our lives should testify of how good God is and we should only be dictated by His ways and precepts. It must have devastated God when Adam took the first bite of the forbitten fruit. It had to frustrate God's kind intent once He saw the images of Himself going about creating their own righteousness. It was disobedient acts that caused God's plans for creation to take a turn for the worst. I say this because everything that He described as very good in the beginning became images that he wanted to destroy. This account was recorded in Genesis 6:1-3 KJV, *"The earth also was corrupt; for all flesh had corrupted His way upon the earth. And God said unto Noah, the end of all flesh is come before Me; for the earth is filled with violence through them; and behold, I will destroy them with the earth."* Now we serve a Righteous Judge and He did not allow sin to go unpunished. He didn't ignore the darkness of the world in the beginning of time and He will not ignore the darkness in this day in time. There is no way of doing the work of intercession operating in darkness. We are called to walk in the Light and to allow our very lives to direct others to the Light.

Shelia R. Pearson

Maintaining a Transformed Life

Once God sanctifies us holy, we must work diligently to maintain our life of holiness. I am a witness that the devil is real and he would love to dwell in the temples that belong to God. After God saved and filled me with His Spirit, I decided to revisit my worldly lifestyle. God had a powerful way of showing me that it was all about being transformed into His image with a mind of never turning back. I must admit that it didn't take God long to draw me back into His presence. Intercessors, once you embrace this work of the Spirit; you cannot divert to a lukewarm lifestyle. You must condition yourselves in this life of holiness. Demons are real and we are called to cast them out, not open a door for them to enter in. It is my prayer that my life helps you truly walk in this life of holiness. We cannot be in God and in the world at the same time.

I tried it and I had a horrible outcome. I shared this life experience in my book *Embracing Intercession Through Life's Experiences*:

"I was having fun doing what I wanted to do and serving God whenever I felt like it. I was the type of believer who lived a lukewarm lifestyle. I will never forget the way God dealt with me about the life I had chosen to live. I was visiting a church and the glory of God filled the sanctuary. Everyone had uplifted hands, but when I attempted to worship God a force kept pushing my hands down. I could literally feel myself fighting the devil to worship God. The more I attempted to raise my hands the stronger this invisible force became. The presence of God felt good and very inviting, but Satan was enjoying my then lukewarm body and wasn't quite ready to give it up. I wanted to experience God's

presence on another level, and I fought until a manifestation of a snake took over my body. I started wiggling uncontrollably all over the church!"

God allowed me to experience this to show me that there is no mixture in this walk with Him. It is His way or the devil's way! We go into ministry proclaiming that we are the called of the Lord. We are best to believe, if God called us, He expects us to truly represent Him.

This is not a life that consist of being partial, it is either you're saved or you're not. You are either righteous or unrighteous. You are either holy or unholy. The Word explains it this way, *"No one who abides in Him [who remains united in fellowship with Him—deliberately, knowingly, and habitually] practices sin. No one who habitually sins has seen Him or known Him. Little children (believers, dear ones), do not let anyone lead you astray. The one who practices righteousness [the one who strives to live a consistently honorable life—in private as well as in public—and to conform to God's precepts] is righteous just as He is righteous."* (1 John 3:6-7 AMP). Intercession is a work that manifests through partnering with a holy God. Once we join ourselves to God to release intercession, we must remain in this posture to continue the work of intercession.

Once we start acting in ways that identify us with the world, we have joined ourselves with the enemy. We cannot work with God and with the enemy at the same time. *"The one who practices sin [separating himself from God, and offending Him by acts of disobedience, indifference, or rebellion] is of the devil [and takes his inner character* and moral values from him, not God]; for the devil have sinned and violated God's law from the beginning. The Son of God appeared for this purpose, to destroy the works of the devil. No one who is born of God [deliberately, knowingly, and habitually] practice sin, because God's seed [His principle of life, the essence of His righteous character remains [permanently] in him [who is born again—who is reborn from above— spiritually transformed, renewed and set apart for His purpose]; and he [who is born again] cannot habitually [live a life characterized by] sin, because he is born of God and longs to please Him. By this the children of God and the children of the devil are clearly identified: anyone who does not practice righteousness [who does not seek God's will in thought, action and purpose] is not of God, nor is the one who does not [unselfishly] love his [believing] brother."* (1 John 3:8-10 AMP).

The person who embraces intercession must understand that holiness is a lifestyle. They must understand that they will never be able to function in the realm of the spirit holding on to worldly tendencies. Intercessors are anointed to keep the devil in his place of defeat and they are never in agreement with his way of doing things. We as believing intercessors must always walk in the essence of God's righteous character. The Bible says, *"Therefore believers, be all the more diligent to make certain about his calling and choosing you [be sure that your behavior reflects and confirms your relationship with God]; for by doing these things [actively developing these virtues], you will never stumble [in your spiritual growth and will live a life that leads others away from sin]."* (2 Peter 1:10 AMP).

From My Heart to Yours

    Over the years I have witnessed a serious falling away of the Kingdom way. The Kingdom way simply means God's way of doing things and what He considers righteous living. People have the tendency to create their own righteousness, but the only thing that will stand before God is true righteousness; the only people that will hear "WELL DONE" are faithful servants. I often hear people say, "But, God know my heart." Yes, He is an All-Knowing God but He will not ignore the fact that you chose sin over righteousness. I know that this truth is not pleasant to everyone, but it will stand when every excuse fails. God is searching for intercessors; He is looking for believers who have given up their own desires for His. It is my prayer that you become the light that draws others into true intercession. I pray that you would release and demonstrate enough light to demolish darkness in all of its forms and manifestations.

Shelia R. Pearson

Chapter 12

The Ongoing Battle

Shelia R. Pearson

    God warns us of the devices of Satan and prepares us for the battles we must fight to maintain our victory in the spirit. If we find ourselves in a defeated state it is not because God has not given us the weaponry that we need to maintain our stand as soldiers. The Bible informs us to make preparation for the enemy by implying that we are to be dressed properly for battle. The strategies and deceits of the devil will be ongoing. Satan will show up with a force to destroy and he will be successful in his attempts if we fail to apply the instructions given by the Word of God. God is giving us fair warning and He is preparing us for all of the deceits of the enemy.   This revelation brings into mind the season my marriage severed. It was an difficult time for me. My family had recently relocated back to our hometown. We quickly found an affordable four-bedroom home. Life appeared to be looking up, but only for a moment. I soon lost the twin boys I was carrying and I found myself on an emotional rollercoaster. During this time, my husband could not do anything right in my eyes. I was the most nagging wife anyone could ever meet. It actually became a lifestyle for me and eventually my husband moved out.

    This was victory for my enemy but it was a throne room experience for me. God began showing me the enemy in every situation. He showed me how I had allowed the enemy to blind me to truth. I was commanded to embrace a consisted prayer life and I was warned by God that if I failed to obey, I would lose everything that I had worked so hard to gain. This was a hard time for me but I had to stay in the face of God to see the tactics of the enemy. God began revealing the strongholds that the enemy was using against me. He was using mind tactics to destroy the love and respect that my husband and I had for one another. God showed me how the enemy had magnified the trivial things to destroy our relationship. I will never forget visiting my husband after we separated. Once I entered the house, I could literally hear the voice of Satan asking me, "*Why are you here?*"

God uncovered the activities that were taking place in the unseen realm and it was a revelation that changed me completely. It was the one moment in time that Ephesians 6:12 became real to me. I had eyes to see and ears to hear where my wrestle was coming from. It was strictly a supernatural battle and I couldn't allow my emotions to dominate. I left my husband's house that day with warfare on my mind. I had seen and heard all that I needed to be placed in the proper posture in the spirit. I understood that it was time for me to maintain a strong stand in the spirit. So, I left my husband's house clothing myself. My feet were being shod with the preparation [to face the enemy with the firm-footed stability, the promptness, and the readiness produced by the good news] of the Gospel of peace.

I was aware of the fact that God had given me everything I needed to be prepared for my enemy. I was dressed and ready to quench all the flaming missiles of the wicked [one] (Ephesians 6:15-16 AMP). I went into spiritual warfare for a time span of about two weeks. I dealt with everything that God had uncovered to me and by the end of that time of warfare, my husband and I were reuniting. The lessons I learned after reconnecting with my husband was that I was fighting an ongoing battle. Once I decided I was tired of fighting, I found myself in divorce court.

Losing my marriage shut me down completely. I found myself losing my identity with no strength left within me to get it back. Life situations had made me numb and getting emotional about anything was a thing of the past. It is amazing how fast certain situations can kill your spiritual drive. God began redirecting me to connect with certain people I had walked away from due to my damaged life. I felt that it was no need of dragging others into my problems. I found myself in a state of feeling totally depleted. I didn't have a desire to pray and prayer was the very thing that defined me. I was in a stagnated place and I found contentment there. I had a powerful prayer ministry that made a tremendous difference in many lives. I also had a completed book that I didn't care to look over and publishing it was not even a thought. I was in a very low place and only the power of God could quicken me. It's not that I was satisfied with my life but I felt like I had found a safe place. I believed that if I wasn't releasing who I was in the spirit, I wouldn't have to deal with the fight that came with it either.

If I didn't think about my book at all, I wouldn't have to stress about how and when I could publish it. If I didn't think about how much I loved and needed my husband, I wouldn't have to humble myself to get my marriage back. I became a person who suppressed my feelings and completely lost my life in the process. I am a chosen intercessor and this vocation requires your spirit to be open to the emotions of God. Without the manifestations that came with this form of prayer, there was no way to be the leader that I was called to be. I had it all wrong when I decided to suppress my emotions. I needed to be emotionally mature to walk successfully as a leader of intercession.

The enemy was aware of my emotional state and he made sure I stayed ignorant of the devices he was using to steal my life. He used my marriage to draw me out of the presence of God. I have learned that he is a clever devil and he targets our personal relationships with the Father. He knew if he could destroy the things that meant the most to me, he could gain total control.

Shelia R. Pearson

Rousing into Action

God is waking us up from a season of rest and He is saying, *"Wake up from sleeping and put actions behind your words!"* If we are not strong enough to be doers of the words which we are speaking, what does those words profit? If we have postured ourselves outside of the will of God, how can we progress in life and ministry? The places we are finding comfort in are cutting us off from the free-flowing lives that God has given us. If we are not progressing, we need to examine our surroundings and shift into our prosperous places to grow. It does not matter if we are connected to a person, a ministry, or a mindset, if it's hindering us, it is time to let it go! Throughout the Bible we are encouraged to strengthen ourselves. We are instructed to, *"Brace up and reinvigorate and set right our slackened and weakened and drooping hands and strengthen our feeble and palsied and tottering knees. And cut through and make firm and plain smooth straight paths for our feet [yes make them safe and upright and happy paths that go in the right direction], so that the lame and halting [limbs] may not be put out of joint, but rather may be cured."*

Notice that we are encouraged to do something about our present state. We are instructed to change our course if it is not leading us to our destiny. It is wise to shift off a normal course if it is not giving us the desired results. Once I realized that my life was diminishing, I had to do something different. I had to make the decision to strengthen myself. I knew if I wanted to see all the many promises that God had shown me, a shift had to take place in my life. It didn't matter how low I felt, I had to tap into the strength that God had made available to me. God is always waiting on us to demonstrate the strength and power He has given us. We are seated in the Lord and nothing in the natural can change who we are in the spirit. God has given us power to defeat the enemy because He has filled us with Himself. We have the All-Powerful God living on the inside of us. It does not matter how the enemy chooses to manifest himself, we are equipped to deal with him. Losing my marriage, ignoring my prayer ministry, and failing to publish a God given book were all manifestations of a weakened state. It was obvious that I was disconnected from my life's source for extremely too long. I had sat in a place of despair for years, allowing the enemy to gain enough ground to separate me from Christ's love; but, the enemy slipped up when he allowed me to get a revelation of Romans 8:34-39 AMP.

This one Word changed my posture in the spirit and this powerful truth is still producing God desired results in my life today. Through this Word I was commanded to examine the situations through the eyes of God. It opens up by questioning me, *"Who is there to condemn [me]? Will Christ Jesus (the Messiah) who died, or rather who was raised from the dead, who is at the right hand of God actually pleading as He intercedes for me? Who shall ever separate me from Christ love? Shall suffering and affliction and tribulation? Or calamity and distress? Or persecution or hunger or destitution or peril or sword? Even as it is written, for my sake I am put to death all the day long; I am regarded as a sheep for the slaughter, yet amid all these things I am more than a conqueror and gain a surpassing victory through Him who love me. For I am persuaded beyond doubt (am sure) that neither death nor life, nor angels nor principalities, nor things impending and threatening nor things to come, nor powers, nor height, nor depth, nor anything else in all creation will be able to separate me from the love of God which is in Christ Jesus my Lord.*" I had to rouse into action by applying God's Word to my life. I had to remind myself of the One who has always made intercession for me. Jesus Christ was my Personal Intercessor and it was time I started acting like He was pleading to the Father on my behalf. Once I changed my posture in the spirit, God gave me my marriage back, I am actively going forth in ministry and you are reading my second published book. I am now enjoying the benefits of my actions only because I shifted out of my weakened state. Yes, we are fighting an ongoing battle but God has given us the arsenal we need to rouse into action and to live out our entire lives victoriously!

From My Heart to Yours

Inspired by 2 Corinthians 4:16-18 AMP

The Father has given us all the love and strength we need to advance in His kingdom. He has empowered us to stand through all situations and circumstances. It is because of His power we have not become discouraged (utterly spiritless, exhausted, and wearied out through fear). Though our outer man is [progressively] decaying and wasting away, yet our inner selves are being [progressively] renewed day by day. For our light, momentary affliction (this slight distress of the passing hour) is ever more and more abundantly preparing and producing and achieving for us an everlasting weight of glory [beyond all measure, excessively surpassing all comparisons and all calculations, a vast and transcendent glory and blessedness never to cease]! Since we consider and look not to the things that are seen but to the things that are unseen; for the things that are visible are temporal (brief and fleeting), but the things that are invisible are deathless and everlasting. It is my prayer that you recognize the power that God has invested within you. And that you learn to see how the enemy is being used to make you stronger. His test and trials are only used to bring you closer and closer into the glory of God. So, I encourage you to start thanking God for allowing the enemy to be used as a tool to make you better.

Shelia R. Pearson

CHAPTER 13

Power to Start and Finish

From start to finish intercession is all about God's intentions. This eliminates the self-will and thrusts you into a supernatural work of the Spirit. The rewarding thing about the proper prayer approach is that you will always get the desired results. It starts as a move of God and it will always manifest in the natural as God's perfect will. Intercession is holy from start to finish and contaminated entrances will only abort the process. No flesh can glory in the presence of God! The one who embraces this life of prayer must first realize that old things have passed away. *"Therefore if anyone is in Christ [that is, grafted in, joined to Him by faith in Him as Savior], he is a new creature [reborn and renewed by the Holy Spirit]; the old things [the previous moral and spiritual condition] have passed away. Behold, new things have come [because spiritual awakening brings new life]."* (2 Corinthians 5:17 AMP).

The one who embraces this life of prayer must also present his or her body as living sacrifices. *"Therefore I urge you, brothers and sisters, by the mercies of God, to present your bodies [dedicating all of yourselves, set apart] as a living sacrifice, holy and well-pleasing to God, which is your rational (logical, intelligent) act of worship. And do not be conformed to this world [any longer with its superficial values and customs] but be transformed and progressively changed [as you mature spiritually] by the renewing of your mind [focusing on godly values and ethical attitudes], so that you may prove [for yourselves] what the will of God is, that which good and acceptable and perfect [in His plan and purposes for you]."* (Romans 12:1-2 AMP). Lastly, the one who embraces this life of prayer must learn of the Word of God because He responds to His Word.

If you plan to see tangible results, it starts with reminding God of His many promises. He is faithful to perform every spoken Word whether we view it as negative or positive. Praying the Word of God is a declaration that says that you trust God to manifest all His precious promises. Jeremiah explains, *"Then the Lord said to me, 'You have seen well, for I am [actively] watching over My word to fulfill it (Jeremiah 1:12 AMP).* The Lord proclaims, *'For I the Lord will speak, and whatever Word I speak will be accomplished. It will no longer be delayed, for in your days, O rebellious house, I will speak the Word and I will fulfill it,' says the Lord God."* (Ezekiel 12:25 AMP).

Seeking God's Will

We often ask ourselves, *"What would Jesus do?"* This shouldn't just become a question to quote, but we should imitate the greatest example ever known to man. He was perfect in all of His ways and He has equipped us with the same level of perfection. Responding as the Great Intercessor must be the life we learn to pursue. Intercession is always spiritual, so we can't function from our soulish nature. This work is too powerful to give our wills, intellects, and emotions free course. How can we birth out God's will if our own heart's desires are overshadowing His heavenly requests? Jesus is our perfect example - He came on the scene looking like, talking like and acting like our heavenly Father. Jesus proclaimed, *"I can do nothing on my own initiative or authority. Just as I hear, I judge; and My judgment is just (fair, righteous, unbiased), because I do not seek My own will, but only the will of Him who sent Me."* (John 5:30 AMP). Birthing the will of God starts with moving according to His instructions. We must rid ourselves of our own desires and embrace the very heart of God.

I mentioned in my first book, *"Embracing Intercession Through Life's Experiences"* how my first assignment started with my mother and sister. I shared how the enemy had a grip on both of their lives. My mother had an alcohol addiction and my sister had cancer. I was instructed to pray for them on a consistent basis and as long as I remained in the right posture, I saw positive results. The minute I allowed my desires to overshadow God's commandments, the enemy came in and destroyed them. The lesson I learned from losing them was that I can't ever function from my soulish nature. I was too emotionally involved to move into true intercession for my family. I stood back in all my acts of selfishness and watched the enemy come in and rob me of my heavenly assignment. We truly have to see the deepness of every assignment given. They are all learning experiences, giving us the advancement we need to do it God's way.

We need God's Spirit and we need His power, but we must learn the simple act of obedience. Our predominate characteristic should always be obedience. Coming into complete compliance with our heavenly instructions is the principle thing. The Bible tells us to *"Prepare our minds for action, be completely sober [in spirit-steadfast, self-disciplined, spiritually and morally alert], fix our hope completely on the grace [of God] that is coming to us when Jesus Christ is revealed. [Live] as obedient children [of God]; do not be conformed to the evil desires which governed us in our ignorance [before we knew the requirements and transforming power of the good news regarding salvation]."* (Peter 1:13-14 AMP). People of God, lives are depending on us to hear the instructions and obey them to the full. The instructions have nothing to do with us but everything to do with the heart of God. If emotions manifest during our times of intercession it is best that they are coming directly from God. It is our job to keep our emotionally disturbed hearts out of the way. If the enemy can keep us functioning in our flesh, he gains ground in our lives. This is victory for him because he is given access to destroy the people we are called to cover in the spirit. If we are busy sobbing about our personal struggles, we will fail at hearing the voice of God. Keep in mind that intercession is all about God's intentions. It is very hard to shift off our heavenly instructions when God really becomes our focus. It does not matter who refuses to follow you or agree with you, your made-up mind places your feet on a path that leads to your destiny. Your eyes will remain fixed on a gaze towards the promise and detours and shortcuts will never be an option. Sometimes you will experience hard times but know that everything you lose wasn't strong enough to take the journey with you. Some things and some people only remained in your life because you compromised. During these times, the world meant more to you than your destiny. A person with a focused mind has embraced the fact that sometimes they will have to walk alone. So, what am I saying? I am informing you that sometimes you will have to lose to gain what matters the most. As you continue to grow in faith, it will require a falling away of past interests and relationships. This process of growth opens doors for you to receive the things needed for the journey ahead.

From My Heart to Yours

The Bible teaches us that we are God's [own] handiwork (His workmanship), recreated in Christ Jesus, [born anew] that we may do those good works which He prearranged and made ready for us to live (Ephesians 2:10 AMP). God is all about us truly representing. He desires to see progress in His kingdom. He graces us with pauses but He would prefer no setbacks. A breather is sometimes needed but we are still expected to keep moving towards the promise. I encourage you to stay focused on God regardless of the many obstacles that are set before you. Know that God has given you all you need to keep walking victoriously in Him. Do your best to stay focused on spiritual matters. The enemy will use those we least expect to distract us. It is his desire to get us off and keep us off the course designed for us. So, maintain your steady gaze towards the promise and refuse to take detours or setbacks. Your goal is to start the course and to finish strong!

Shelia R. Pearson

Conclusion

A Kingdom Display

I have learned that my role as an apostolic intercessor is so important to the kingdom of God and I pray that you know that your role is just as important. God has given us gifts and talents to advance His kingdom. It is imperative that we release our gifts in full confidence knowing that they are empowered to save souls. We shouldn't ever limit our abilities in the spirit because others can't agree. There is no other soul capable of feeling the burden of what God has placed on the inside of us. At all times we should acknowledge the God who cared enough to give His only begotten Son so that we could be numbered among the chosen. We are taught that God selected (deliberately chose) what in the world is foolish to put wise to shame (1Corinthians 1:27 AMP).

We were not chosen because we had it all together. I am certain that God didn't choose me because I was the wisest of the wise. I believe I was chosen because I was one of the weakest among my peers. Now as I stand before God's people releasing the unadulterated truth, He gets the glory. God is glorified even the more through the weakest vessel. I can glory in the fact that the All-Powerful God *"selected (deliberately chose) what, in the world, is lowborn, insignificant, branded and treated with contempt - even the things that are nothing, that He might dispose and bring to nothing the things that are, so that no mortal man should [have pretense for glorying and] boast in the presence of God."* (1 Corinthians 1:28 AMP). All praises must be given to God. It is His equipping power that gives us the results we need. It is His strong arm that gives us the strength that we need; and simply put, it is His righteousness that put our lives in right standing with Him.

We are taught that a man's gift makes room for him and brings him before great men (Proverbs 18:16 AMP). We are filled with the light of the Gospel to shine bright in this world and we must take on an attitude of refusing to hold back. God continues to remind us of our value and we must maintain focus when it comes to who we are for Him. I will never forget the season that God began dealing with me about my first book. I had published it but I had no drive when it came to promoting it. God wanted me to understand that writing and publishing a book meant nothing if I wasn't confident enough to promote it. He did not give me His wisdom for it to remain hidden within. The power of God must always flow freely in this world and it is vital that we view ourselves the same way Jesus viewed His disciples. He encouraged them by letting them know that they are the salt of the earth.

He proclaimed, *"You are the salt of the earth; but if the salt has lost its taste (purpose), how can it be made salty? It is no longer good for anything, but to be thrown out and walked on by people [when the walkways are wet and slippery]. You are the light of [Christ to] the world. A city set on a hill cannot be hidden; nor does anyone light a lamp and put it under a basket, but on a lampstand, and it gives light to all who are in the house. Let your light shine before men in such a way that they may see your good deeds and moral excellence, and [recognize and honor and glorify your Father who is in heaven."* (Matthew 5:13-14 AMP). Jesus is letting us know that our gifts were given to bring glory to God and they must be put on display.

A Display of Faith

God has empowered us to work great exploits for His kingdom and we really need to see this truth. It is so important that we see just how gifted we are and began functioning in that power. There is no way of operating according to God's plan for our lives if we don't recognize the difference we are empowered to make. The Word states that each of us has received a gift (a particular spiritual talent, a gracious divine endowment). The Word goes on to encourage us to employ it for one another as [befits] good trustees of God's many-sided grace [faithful stewards of the extremely diverse powers and gifts granted to Christians by unmerited favor] (1 Peter 4:10 AMP). This Scripture paints an image of how special we are and it is vital that we know that whatever gift or talent that God has made known to us, it is empowered to make a difference in the world.

We must recognize who we are according to God's plan for our lives and agree with it through works of obedience. It takes faith to really see the truth about yourself. It even takes faith to believe that God has gifted us to make an impact in this world. This is why faith must become priority in our lives. I entitled this topic, "*A Display of Faith*" and anything that is placed on display is put in a place to be seen at all times. It does not matter the season - it is always within plain view. This is how faith should be presented. Even though seasons change, our faith should always remain the same. Faith consist of a lot of things but wavering is not one of them. God is always God and it is either we trust Him or we don't. I will never forget the Word God dropped in the spirit of my husband and I during a time of testing. God had blessed us with a great business and it was going well. God had given us an increase but during this time of brightness, darkness tried to overshadow us. The test was so intense that my husband began speaking words of defeat. It seemed as if my words of encouragement weren't reaching his heart. Discouragement seemed to grow bigger and bigger in our car that day. I then heard the Lord instructing me to turn the radio on. I obeyed and God magnified Himself greater than anything the enemy was trying. The voice of Maurette Brown Clark encouraging me that it wasn't over until GOD said it was! God lifted a standard that day that commanded us to recognize that He was in control. The enemy will never have the power to shift the promises of God and it is our job to stand on faith regardless of the test.

We have to always acknowledge the fact that God is allowing our faith to be tested and He allows this for our benefit. God is our security and even when things come up against us, our faith must be a faith that remains. The Bible teaches us that, *"Now faith is the assurance (title deed, confirmation) of things hoped for (divinely guaranteed), and the evidence of things not seen [the conviction of their reality—faith comprehends as fact what cannot be experienced by the physical senses]. For by this [kind of] faith men of old gained [divine] approval."* (Hebrews 11:1-2 AMP). It is important that we understand that God created us to display His kingdom. He needs us to operate in faith when it comes to our gifts and talents and know that this is how we will gain divine approval just like the men of old.

Shelia R. Pearson
From My Heart to Yours

It is my prayer that you know that your display of faith is a display of the power of God. He is the only Light that can shine bright enough to destroy the works of the devil. There is nothing too hard for God and you should always declare this truth. Think about this, if you never experience hard times how can you say you serve a way maker. If you never experience sickness how can you testify that God is a healer. Learn to go through your difficult times so that you can really shine as a son of God. Also keep in mind that your victories in the spirit will always put God on display.

Advancing for Kingdom Sake!

About the Author

Shelia R. Pearson is the founder of The Anointed Gap Standers' Ministries; a multi-cultural mission to bring the ligaments and joints of Christ's Body back together. Shelia has also authored another title, *"Embracing Intercession Through Life's Experiences."* She travels, doing evangelistic ministry, and has a vision to teach, train, and activate intercession and spiritual warfare.

She lives in Cordova, TN with her husband, Keith Pearson, Sr. and her three wonderful children: Kelvineisha, Kimberly, and Keith Jr..

Made in the USA
Monee, IL
03 May 2021